Folds to the Door

A History of Camp Hagan

Shawnee-on-Delaware

1937-1970

Alice Royer Roy

Folds to the Door is both a historical work and a memoir collaboration; all materials referenced may be found in the Endnotes at the conclusion of each chapter as well as the Works Cited at the end of this book.

Published in the United States

ISBN: 978-1-937588-72-4

Formatted by Stephanie Lynn Blackman
Whitman, MA

For Peg, who loved summer camp in Michigan,
Joey, who liked nature study at day camp, but not the bus
ride or the mosquitoes,
and Bill, who listened to my camp stories, read drafts,
wrangled photos and fancy tech things, and unfailingly
showed me the forest for the trees.

And for all my Hagan sisters…

Acknowledgments

First, thanks to Robin Fidler Brancato who read, edited, (and cajoled me ever so gently to trim) these pages so as to bring to light the history of our camp, along with the memories we hold dear. Robin always asked the right questions and offered encouragement at the right times. Any errors, of course, are my responsibility.

Also, I thank editor/publisher Stephanie Blackman of Riverhaven Books. I entrusted her with our dream and she came through for us with attentive and creative responses. She did us proud.

Many of the eldest campers contributed with their memories as well as their encouragement, especially Chris Hill Killough.

Then thanks especially to Ruth Clegg Whitsel, Pat Ulrich Ritter, and the late Phyllis Wiest Gilbert who interviewed several directors and early campers. Pat and Phyl went to the Lutheran Seminary in Philadelphia and gained permission to photocopy the pertinent Synod *Minutes*, information that was hugely important in helping me, for all of us, to know what was going on behind the scenes. Ruth, I couldn't have done it without you, remembering, emailing every day, cheering me on when I felt overwhelmed.

To my counselors and friends Inge Woerman Coleman and Midge Wilkinson Vansant, thank you for your wisdom and loving kindness to those of us lucky enough to grow under your guidance and then to have you as our role models when we were counselors.

I regret that I can't name every one of the many alums who talked to me by email, sent memorabilia, and/or filled out questionnaires. Your generosity and enthusiasm were always inspiring. And thanks to all who contributed a little extra to production and mailing costs. I appreciate you all so very much.

The book of nature is always open.

Esther M. Wenrich,
The Staffing of Public Elementary School Camps

Table of Contents

Foreword

If you're reading this sentence, chances are you're one of the many boosters, groupies, survivors of the now almost mythic Camp Hagan at Shawnee-on-Delaware. Or else you're a deprived, never-went-to-Hagan relative or friend who's being handed this book in order to prove to you what you missed. The happy outcome of a certain conversation at a 2009 reunion has resulted in Alice Royer Roy's taking up the challenge of writing this history. So here we are, with her chronological account of Hagan, divided into beginning, middle and end. But of course there is no end, as Alice suggests in her epilogue, as long as even one of us manages to keep a single camp memory alive.

Folds to the Door is primarily a recollection of priceless memories, but you have a choice in your approach to reading it. You can concentrate so thoroughly that you'll know the name of the carpet manufacturing company run by Peter Paul Hagan, donor of the land where all this happened, or else, you can skim thirteen chapters plus appendices, just hoping to see your own name come up. You'll find a lot of research, explanation, and insight into theories and practices of camping, education, and culture of the time, and besides that, a lot of more mundane bits, such as the lyrics to "Bless 'em all, bless 'em all."

The first season of Hagan was in 1937, the final one in 1970. Each of our personal perceptions of camp may depend on where we landed on that timeline. Some of us made it to camp in spite of gas rationing in the W.W.II years. Others experienced summers through the prism of sixties' assassinations and protests. For many, though, regardless of personal troubles or chaos in the world, Hagan was Shangri-La-- a permanently happy land isolated from the outside, where, as the song goes, we "let the rest of the world go by."

Were we naïve or just plain lucky to have had that benign interlude? Or, without realizing it, were we being prepared for the future by the camp's stated goals?. I'm talking about: socially broaden, physically fortify, and spiritually deepen. As examples, those collaborative skits, Miller dances, and whispered confidences after taps. Those tournaments, playdays, and nearly sadistic cold dips in the Delaware. Those dewy evenings in the outdoor chapel that could spiritually deepen an atheist.

Somehow or another, along with all those experiences, plus the modelling and inspiration of good, encouraging, hard-working counselors and administrators, most of us ended up with a permanent Hagan stamp on us, an invisible tattoo. Or, as Sandy Dempsey is quoted as saying somewhere in these pages: "Oh, this camp of ours. How it has a hold on us."

Thanks to Alice and all who contributed to committing our story to print.

Robin Fidler Brancato

Introduction

You mean, you went to camp all summer long?
And you went BACK?
a non-camper

People without camp experience find it hard to believe that longtime campers spent many summers at camp, frequently as campers and then as counselors. On the other hand, longtime campers can hardly believe that anybody else wouldn't have wanted to do just that. How can anyone not imagine that a girl or boy might wait through the school year for camp to start again? But for those of us who did, Hagan has remained a formative part of our lives, and we can't imagine ourselves without it. The three main goals of Camp Hagan – to socially broaden, physically fortify, and spiritually deepen – were realized in our lives.

Camp Hagan flourished in the Pocono Mountains, north of Shawnee-on-Delaware, from 1937 to 1970. Many years later, in 2009, a reunion of some sixty campers and counselors from the 1930s, '40s, and '50s was hosted by Carolyn McGonigle Holleran in Sinking Spring, Pennsylvania. Although reunions had been taking place for decades, at this gathering some camper/counselors from the '40s and '50s, who had just been found by the elder group, were included, and I was happily one of them. At that reunion someone said, "Oh, I wish we had a history of Hagan," and I took on the task. After that, Pat Ulrich Ritter found the '60s alums online and we were thus able to make our book about the whole life of Camp Hagan.

Many camp alumnae speak of "joy" – their joy in camping, in living, playing, and learning with the other girls, in being at Camp Hagan. This book chronicles the underpinnings and the atmosphere of that joy. Through this story we get a glimpse of a way of life that's gone – camp life, the mid-century towns campers came from, and the parents who sent their daughters. It opens a window on a particular time, which had not occurred before and would end a few decades after. This period brought, as well, a remarkable confluence of social change and developments in the psychology of learning.

Much of my joy in working on this book has come out of the connections now forged among so many former campers and counselors among the eldest, the middle group, and the last generation of alumnae. Through interviews, responses to questionnaires, and constant email correspondence, I have discovered how Hagan launched the lives of those who attended and how much Camp Hagan remains part of people's lives, fifty or sixty or more years after they first set foot on campus.

Of course, not everyone loved camp. One acquaintance of mine went to camp in Illinois for one year and hated it. In *A Manufactured Wilderness*, author Abigail Van Slyck speaks of herself as "a failed camper," at first just too homesick to continue at camp[1], and dedicates her book to her parents, who "sent me to camp until I liked it."

But many people's eyes light up when the topic of camping arises, and we know we're drawing on the same (almost) inexpressible knowledge: why we loved our camp.

There are not many original sources to provide facts for an examination of early summer camps. Most directors did not keep detailed records and, if they did, they didn't hang onto them after they stopped being directors. Most letters home have been long since discarded, and, because early camps were largely unregulated, there is no repository of reports to agencies or other official groups. Many early details are thus lost.

To recover some of this information about camp life, we can go to the people who lived it, or be lucky and diligent enough to uncover a stash of history hidden away. Fortunately, we have both. This book is based on approximately one-hundred-twenty responses to questionnaires sent to Camp Hagan campers and counselors, as well as interviews with directors, along with materials and memorabilia which they provided. And, thanks to the efforts of Pat Ulrich Ritter and Phyllis Wiest Gilbert, this history also draws on the annual minutes of the Eastern Pennsylvania Lutheran Synod, dealing with the business side of the camp and showing the board's belief in the role of camping for girls.

A major source for the early years has been a gold-mine album containing daily activities kept by early directors or assistant directors, known as the *Wooden Album*, or the Hagan Scrapbook. Finally, sources for this book include the synod's promotional brochures for Hagan, campers' memory books, camp newssheets, published works about summer camps, conversations with people who went to other camps in many parts of the country, and, of course, my own memories and experiences at Camp Hagan. (Details of sources appear in Headwaters.)

Talking with people who went to camps all over the country affirms what the published sources say about American summer camps: while there are, of course, differences among camps – in part due to geography or time – the similarity of traditions and practices is astounding. What was singular was the place of such camps in the American landscape in 20th century American history.

Summer camps arose as part of a general impulse in early and mid-20th century society to enrich children's lives by exposing them to nature. However, summer camps also reflected the belief that this goal would best be accomplished in groups set off by certain boundaries, based on being a girl or a boy, Protestant or Jewish, black or white, or inner city, and so on. That social motivation would change with the Civil Rights movement and a greater value later placed on diversity and inclusion – but not yet. Camp Hagan was a space inhabited mainly by middle-class white girls, the vast majority Protestants, and most of them Lutheran.

Besides giving former campers and counselors a welcome trip down Memory Lane, this investigation is a kind of case study in which I am both a participant (past) and an observer (present). Knowing that memories are not always reliable, they fade and warp with time, I have included only material drawn from existing written Hagan sources or, in the case of campers' individual memories (and my own), confirmed by at least one other source.

Several years ago, at the beginning of my research on the history of Camp Hagan, I told collaborators who were interviewing older campers and former directors that I wanted *everything* they could get. I now understand the advice to be careful what you wish for. I have been gloriously inundated with data – computer files, hard copy files, notes from research, notes from correspondence with campers from the beginning to the end. It has been a wonderful immersion, and I don't regret a minute of it. In the end, though, I couldn't possibly use everything. I've had to select facts and stories from the wealth of contributions to tell our story.

This book tells the story of the life of a summer camp and of camp life as many of us lived it during the thirty-four years of its existence. First, a look at camping in general will provide us with a grounding to understand one particular camp more clearly. After a short foray back into geological time, when the land that housed Camp Hagan was formed, we will reimagine the events and daily lives and traditions of this camp during its brief sojourn on the bank of the Delaware. At the end, the book comes full circle, to the irony of the Tock's Island Dam project, returning once again to the land.

Let Barb Belon speak for us: *We will be eternally grateful to the founders, the LCA, and the counselors/staff that gave us so much.*

(adapted)

Endnotes

---

[1] "failed camper" Van Slyck, p. xv; "until I liked it" p. v

Part I: The Beginning

Chapter 1

Early History of American Summer Camps

There was an American summer camp movement,
and we were part of it. Who knew? Not us.

Why Did Summer Camps Start?

Camp life is hard to capture in words. Many Hagan campers have voiced this lament, as have campers from all eras, from all parts of the country. Similarly, almost every writer about camps, whether in scholarly text or memoir, says the same thing. Then they proceed to try, and so do we, to grasp the essence of our experiences and affection through facts and memories. To understand fully our own lives at camp, it will be helpful to understand the camping scene that Hagan entered. And to do that, we need to look back to when it all began.[2]

Campsites appear in 19th century paintings and later photographs at fishing and hunting grounds and, of course, in the Civil War and other military locations. These may be considered "necessary" camping, compared with recreational camping that gave rise to camps such as Hagan and many others. The earliest recorded recreational camp, called the Gunnery, in Connecticut, was founded in 1861, but it didn't apparently lead to any continuation or development of camps. Recreational camping got its true start in the 1880s and 1890s, with a few camps serving middle- and upper-class Protestant boys when some dedicated teachers and outdoorsmen took small groups of young teenage boys to the lakes and woods in Maine and New Hampshire.

From this small start grew a project of astonishing dimensions. One of three trends was the new concept of the annual holiday. What came to be called a "vacation" in urban areas became a marker of social status. The second trend was the change in children's schedules. For children who went to school, there used to be a regular summer term, but during the late 19th century, schools began closing for summer vacation. On farms and in working class urban areas, children worked, but the middle-class and affluent families now had children at home for the summer. A third trend was a change in attitude toward the imagined shape of childhood, now seen as a carefree time, in which, at least in the middle and upper classes, children were freed from work. However, the free time of vacation had its downside. Adults did not want children running around loose, getting into trouble. They wanted that time to be enjoyable and productive, through activities that would both strengthen and educate. Boys' camps would be first, as girls were still safe at home.

Along with these social trends, beliefs of adults at the end of the 19th century also affected the development of summer camps and the forms they took. Anxieties about the condition of the modern world underlay many of these beliefs. One concern was that people in offices all day, as well as children in schools, were losing, or had lost, earlier virtues of the pioneers – bravery, independence, resourcefulness, and an ability to survive without soft modern conveniences. The modern world seemed to exist mainly in cities, and cities had dangers – disease and crime in particular. The cities also demonstrated the changing face of the population through immigration, new arrivals who presumably didn't share early American history and ideals. That history and those ideals were not so far away – after all, at the turn of the last century, America was only 125 years old. So, a rural environment was seen as better for children to develop in, at least in the new two or three months of available vacation time.

Another early modern anxiety was more gender-specific. This worry took the shape of distress about the coddling of boys by over-protective, over-indulgent mothers, leading to the enfeebling of men. Camp could channel boys' normal adventurous trouble-making by providing a peer group of older boys under men's guidance for physical, outdoor activity and character development. The nature that they would spend their summers in would not be wild, but controlled and safe. In effect, a managed wilderness full of the images of a wonderful recuperative space and time.

So, adult anxieties about the modern world – dirty, crowded, dangerous cities, and the sense that women were feminizing generations of boys into soft, effeminate men – made the wilderness lifestyle of an imagined earlier time seem like a solution to these problems.

In the 19th century, the national goal was to close the frontier, to eradicate untamed wilderness in favor of control and productivity.[3] It was felt that the "Indians" had failed to make the land productive and so didn't deserve to have it. In the late 19th century, however, this view changed. People came to see the wilderness as precious, a place where city dwellers might revive and renew their spirits.

Summer camps grew out of this change in attitude: an appreciation of wilderness and fear of loss of the wild parts of nature. This explains, in part, why at the turn of the century summer camps were mainly in the East, and Northeast especially: that's where most of the big cities were, and big cities were the clear antithesis of the wilderness. In the Mid-West and West, people already lived near or had access to lakes, woods, and mountains. There were fewer big cities, and those that existed weren't as big as those on the East Coast. Those cities were newer, too, and the land was not as built up, not so filled.

By contrast, many people along the Eastern seaboard wanted to get their children out of the cities and "back" into the wilderness, which now had to be reconstructed for them. Large tracts of farmland were in a sense reclaimed, transformed back into an imagined version of wilderness and oriented toward recreational use.

Indians, Pioneers, and Soldiers

It was pretty much agreed that the wilderness life of an earlier time would offer the rugged, primitive experience to boys that would enable them to grow into strong, manly men. But how would that wilderness life be achieved?

Two themes of early-American life encapsulated the hopes and aspirations of adults for children's time at camp – pioneer life and "American Indian" life. These ideals would dictate what the content of early camp life could be. In 1901, a camping group called Woodcraft Indians was established, and 1905 saw the founding of the Sons of Daniel Boone. At the start of the 20th century, the view that camp life should focus on the lore and practices of the indigenous peoples prevailed over the nostalgia for pioneer life. It seemed to resonate more with people's anti-modern anxieties.

Camps were often given Indian names, such as Kehonka [4], Mishawaka, and Lohican (in the Poconos). Some of these names were local to the area where the camp was established, some had historical references, sometimes they were just made up to sound Indian. Such names gave the impression that the land had gone directly from the Natives to the camp owners. Often a barn wall or some other sign of the area's previous incarnation as a farm would remain, clearly not part of the original wilderness.

At camps with a strong Indian focus, boys were taught Indian chants, dances, lore, and nature craft. Most early camps started out as tents, but even after they moved to cabins, there would be a tipi in a prominent place, surrounded with Indian artifacts, some authentic, many made by the campers. Much of the lore, artifacts, and rituals were derived from the Plains Indians, far from the locations of the early camps, and were mixed with stories and practices of Indians of the Northeast. All camps appear to have had council fires. Early "necessary" campsites (fishing and hunting campsites or military encampments) had campfires, of course, but the label of council fire was specifically drawn from real or imagined Indian life. Boys wore headbands with feathers and special Indian-esque robes for ceremonies.

Middle- and upper-class boys, it seemed, were approaching a manhood that was threatened by over-civilization and feminized homes; it failed to develop the self-reliance that people believed had characterized earlier generations, especially the pioneers. As enthusiasm for approximating Indian life in camps waned, interest in learning pioneer virtues increased. In the 1920s actual log cabins were constructed, later giving way to plainly built wooden cabins. Campers

5

learned woods craft under the heading of Pioneering. Thus, one of the main ways to rescue children from the dangers and unwholesome air of the cities so they could become stronger, more independent, and self-reliant men was through a romanticized reproduction of frontier life, away from modern comforts and technologies. Activities such as fishing, building fires, cooking over open fires, handicrafts, and sleeping in cabins became some of the means to accomplish these goals.

After WWI, most camps had both cabins, suggestive of pioneer life, and council fire rings, in imagined imitation of Indian life. Then a military theme was added.

The Boy Scouts was founded in England in 1908 as a response to the ill-preparedness of British soldiers in the Boer War. This was a critique of working-class home life, but when, in the 1910s, the Boy Scouts expanded into North America, the attack was aimed at middle- class mothers for raising perfect gentlemen and inhibiting boys' natural growth into robust manhood. Getting boys out into nature with manly Christians was determined to be a solution. The Scouting organization shared the current enthusiasms for both Native American and pioneer nostalgia, with the added influence of military authority, patriotism, and preparedness for war[5].

In the late 19th century, the earliest camps, generally wealthy private camps, were usually collections of tents in a wooded area, dotted naturally among the trees. However, in the early 20th century, military encampments became the model for camp layout. There would be a square parade ground, with tents around three sides, or in a semi-circle, or in rows. Military practices took place in the parade ground – reveille, flag raising, cannon salutes, calisthenics, taps. Uniforms were modeled on what was known as "military drab," and meals were eaten in the mess tent.

In the 1920s, however, the military came to be associated with inflexibility rather than good discipline. The horrors of the recent war also contributed to this reduction in confidence that having children in military-like environments, engaging in soldiering practices, would lead to better men and women in the next generation.

What About the Girls?

The Victorian era saw tight control of young women in dress, education, and activities. At the end of the 19th century, employment in factories, stores, and offices opened opportunities, though for poor women these "opportunities" were often found in garment-making sweat shops. However, middle-class women began to teach school, and colleges began to admit upper-class young women. Less identified with home and hearth, women were out working for women's right to vote, going to college, entering the professions, and participating in sports and outdoor activities. New girls' camp directors were mostly educated middle-class women who saw themselves equally as able as men in politics, professions, and higher education.

The first girls' camp was started in 1902 in Maine. By 1910 there were forty-one, all in New England. By 1915, there were one hundred. Although large numbers of early camps lasted only a few years, most continued into the 1920s, and camping expanded into North Carolina, Michigan, Wisconsin, Iowa, Colorado, and Washington.

Early girls' camps were fairly informal and did not have much of an organized daily program. There was an emphasis on arts and creativity, as well as the chance to learn sports, water skills, and campcraft – to learn things girls would not have had the chance to learn at home. Indeed, this effect would carry forward throughout all of summer camps' history: that girls could learn and do things we would not have been able to learn and do at home.

Most camps stayed somewhat plain, if not primitive then at least rustic. A few camps became quite luxurious, with a cook, white linen tablecloths, and table service, but this approach to camping was not widespread and did not last long.

At the beginning, attendance of girls at summer camps was not looked on with favor. And there were restrictions on girls' participation in camping rituals that did not apply to boys. For example, while boys wore feathered headdress in their Indian ceremonial dances, early photos show girls in headbands but no feathers – feathers were only for braves. In some early camps, one of the boys' duties was to check the primitive sanitation systems and arrange for any needed repairs. When girls made such rounds of the sanitation areas, their main job was to clean.   The Sons of Daniel Boone, founded in 1905, were joined in the 1910s by the Girl Pioneers of America, founded by the sisters of the founder of the Sons of Daniel Boone. Boys were to be strong, with lofty aims and strong character. Girls were to develop strength, honesty, and self-sacrifice. Boys were not expected to be unselfish or self-sacrificing. And self-sufficiency for girls was not widely seen to be a good thing.

The great advance in girls' and young women's clothing was bloomers! These "bifurcated garments" allowed girls to hike, climb, and play sports, unencumbered with long skirts and petticoats. There was disapproval and some ridicule about this attire, but there was no turning back. Girls' camps had arrived to stay. By 1915, one camp's brochure proclaimed, "Camp life for girls is no longer an experiment."[6]

Not One Size Fits All

As the small number of camps in the 1880s began to multiply, American summer camps became the summer camp industry, serving many other constituencies than the several hundred middle- and upper-class Protestant boys with which it began; girls, new immigrants, and members of religious, political, and sometimes racial minorities [7] attended. By the interwar years (between WWI and the end of WWII), more than a million children each summer attended thousands of camps[8] across the country.

Camps can be divided into a few types. The main division is simply between private camps and organizational camps. At the beginning of organized camping, all camps were individually owned and operated. Most of these, as we have seen, were in New England, serving upper-class white Protestant boys, and later girls. For the northern elite, attending summer camp became an expected rite of passage, so that by

1930, two-thirds of incoming students at Vassar had been to camp[9].

But by the turn of the century, the summer camp movement was growing rapidly, and "organizational" camps sponsored by social service agencies and youth organizations were rapidly appearing. The first organizational camps were sponsored by groups such as Boy Scouts and Girl Scouts and YM- and YWCAs. Founded by men known as "muscular Christians," the first YMCA camps defined their success not only through evidence of physical strengthening but also by the number of religious conversions achieved at campfires.

YMCA, Girl Scouts, Boy Scouts, Camp Fire Girls, and similar groups had different goals and a different structure from the early elite private camps. For middle-class children from cities and suburbs, these organizational camps were more affordable, and campers could go for shorter sessions, to places more easily reached by train. Counselors at YM- and YWCAs were Y workers, taking their own vacation to work at the camps. Recruiting was done at rallies at the Y in the spring, and a national organization supplied camp activities, methods, and building plans.

Church-sponsored camps joined the burgeoning development of summer camps, functioning for the most part without state or national coordination. They shared the YMCA's goals, but some were less overtly evangelical, defined more through attendance by children of the religious group than by campfire conversions. The yearly records for Camp Hagan and Camp Miller show that the Lutheran synod fathers kept a careful count of the ratio of Lutheran to non-Lutheran campers, noting in 1941 "an encouraging increase in the number of Lutheran" campers. In 1947, campers at Hagan were 75% Lutheran, staff 52%. Most every year for the rest of its existence saw this kind of accounting. Campers who were not Lutheran (and they were counted, too) were of the major Protestant denominations: Presbyterian, Episcopal, Methodist, Reformed, and later UCC.

Individual camps, both private and organizational, were largely segregated spaces, reflecting particular constituencies that provided

9

ethnic, racial, and religious homogeneity. By the early 20th century, boys and girls, recent immigrants and native-born, children of union activists, socialists, and progressive educators, Protestants, Jews, and Catholics, all races and classes were going to camp, though not usually together.

A third kind of camp, which could be considered another kind of organizational camp, were charitable, or agency, camps: think the New York Herald-Tribune Fresh Air Camps, which have lasted through the 20th century and into the 21st, with the purchase of the *Herald-Tribune* by the *New York Times*. While the goal of early private camps was to toughen the elite, the goals of charitable camps were to uplift the poor and Americanize new immigrants. Some charitable camps sought an ethnic mix of children with a view to making the American melting pot theory real. But some parents didn't like their children mixing with campers from other ethnic groups. Jews and Italian immigrants were often excluded. Then, as other religious, ethnic, and immigrant groups became more established and affluent, they started their own summer camps, with overt or implied restrictions like those of the private camps.

* * *

Although the summer camp model was transported to many parts of the world, children's summer camps began in the United States and were most successful there. As children's camps grew in numbers, so did a consistent idea of what the summer camp experience would include: living in groups, away from parents but with adult leadership, spending most of the time outdoors, developing skills and appreciation for nature, and sitting around campfires[10]. Camp rituals that are well over a century old were initiated in the very early years.

Adults expected camp to provide a return to natural wilderness living, an escape from city dangers. But children did not share their parents' urban anxieties. At camp, children learned nostalgia for things that belonged to previous generations, that they were too young to remember[11]. The camper's day was filled with activities which adults might hope would engender in children their own nostalgia for past wilderness or frontier life. While the idea of a summer camp experience

10

was greatly influenced by adults' anti-modern anxieties as well as their hopes for their children's well-being and healthy development, it was the children who actually lived the experience and took away with them values and memories beyond what adults may have imagined.

Endnotes

---

[2] This chapter draws heavily – and gratefully – on two sources: Leslie Paris's *Children's Nature* and Abigail Van Slyck's *A Manufactured Wilderness*. I hope this "blanket footnote" will suffice to suggest how much I and the camping world owe Paris and Van Slyck for their contribution to our understanding of summer camps.

[3] p. 3

[4] Kahn, p. 5 and Paris, p. 19

[5] Van Slyck, p. 18

[6] p. 49

[7] Paris, p. 3

[8] p. 3

[9] Paris, p. 6

[10] Paris, p. 12

[11] Paris, p. 13

Chapter 2

Hopes and Plans

...ever thankful...
Barb Belon

The building of Camp Hagan reflected the personal dreams of its founders at the same time as it brought together broader social concerns. But making a vision into reality requires hard work, cooperation, and funding.

Thus, in 1935 and 1936, the Lutheran Ministerium of Pennsylvania, a synod of the national Lutheran church, voiced their hopes and aspirations, goals and expectations, for a new girls' camp through a sales brochure. The 1937 pamphlet, produced during the winter (well ahead of the actual camping season so as to be available in church offices), was full of attractive descriptions of facilities and activities and necessary information for prospective campers and their parents. In the two years before the opening of Camp Hagan, hopes and plans were also revealed in the synod's annual minutes, which recorded business details as well as the synod leaders' purpose and expectations for the new camp. These two sources tell us much about the origin of Camp Hagan.

In 1935 the Evangelical Lutheran Ministerium of Pennsylvania and the Adjacent States began talking about a girls' camp that would offer to Lutheran girls the same opportunities Camp Miller, the brother camp, had been offering to boys since its establishment in 1922. To this end the Youth Activities committee "sought to gather information and material in reference to a girls' camp" (Lutheran *Minutes* 1936). We could wish to know what that information and material were, but there is no record of their sources.

To be sure, there was camp information out in the public arena which the Synod may well have accessed. An early camping association, the

National Association of Directors of Girls' Camps, merged with a boys' camp association and became the well-known and fairly influential Camp Directors Association. The official industry journal *Camping*, along with *Camping World* and *Camp Life*, provided insight into current camp practices and problems. The popular *Redbook* magazine had a whole camping department.

For models, the Synod had at least two: the early Lutheran camp in central Pennsylvania – Camp Nawakwa at Biglerville, north of Gettysburg – and Camp Miller's fifteen years of experience. They certainly drew on that cumulative knowledge, along with the leadership of LeRoi Snyder, who in 1936 served as Field Secretary of Muhlenberg College and Camps Director.

Due in part to the popularity of Camp Miller for boys, the Ministerium and parents wanted, as the 1937 sales brochure put it, a fine girls' camp "within the reach of the average family's budget." Legend has it that E. Clarence Miller and Peter Paul Hagan[12] were friendly competitors at their Lutheran church in Philadelphia, St. John's in Melrose Park. In 1927 Clarence Miller had donated land along the Delaware River in the Poconos for a boys' camp, previously located along the Perkiomen since 1922 – Camp Miller. Not to be outdone, the story goes, Peter Paul Hagan, in 1936, donated land for a girls' camp, a few miles upriver. If this was competition, it was a leisurely one, taking a decade to materialize. In any case, many boys and girls were the lucky beneficiaries.

Camp Miller had the better waterfront – shallower water, less current, and a lower embankment. Camp Hagan, on the deepest-channel side of the river at that point, had a more severe drop-off, strong current, and a high, steep bank separating the campus from the river. However, Miller, with easier access to the water, was flooded twice over the years of its existence and Hagan not at all, so perhaps the contest was a tie.

Plans for the girls' camp moved quickly. The 1937 *Minutes* tell us that the camp, donated by Mr. and Mrs. Peter Paul Hagan of Philadelphia, and funded by the Lutheran Ministerium, would be four miles north of Camp Miller, on 32.6 acres of land, with 1500 feet of frontage on the

Delaware and ten acres of woodland. However, the sales brochure for 1937 (and always after that) stated there were twenty-seven acres.

Building started in October 1936 and continued in the spring of 1937, when the weather improved.

The maximum capacity expected would be two hundred campers per week, though in the first season there were to be no more than eighty-four campers in any week. According to the Lutheran *Minutes*, there would be twelve "cottages," as the cabins were initially called, as well as an office building and an infirmary. The *Minutes* also stated that the campus would feature a dining hall and kitchen and two shower houses. Through the Hagans' donation and the added financial support of the Ministerium, the 1937 *Minutes*, before the opening season, reported "Camp Hagan has become a reality."

According to the 1936 *Minutes*, Camp Miller was "A Real Camp For Real Boys," and the Ministerium's mission for Miller was "to develop Christian manhood" in the boys who went there. For Camp Hagan girls the objectives were "to spiritually deepen, to socially broaden, and to physically fortify." Although later Hagan Memory Books show that

Gladys Marie Staub of Scranton PA. Graduated from Susquehanna University, Bachelor of Science, and from Johns Hopkins Training School for Nurses. General Obstetrical Staff of the Women's Clinic, Johns Hopkins Hospital Asst. Supervisor Pediatric Dispensary of the Harriet Lane Home In charge of Metabolism Ward of the Osler Clinic

Hagan was to be known as "A Camp with Character," the 1938 Lutheran *Minutes* report that Hagan truly was a "Camp with *a* Character." More than one, as campers through the years might say; always more than one!

15

The new camp's staff, according to the 1937 sales brochure, would be "young women of fine Christian character who have had experience in camping" and brought some specialty to the camp program. The starting plan was for a ratio of one counselor to seven campers, with five counselors on the supervisory staff.

A page in the sales brochure, sent to parents after their daughter was registered at Camp Hagan, was entitled "Important Camp Information." Here campers and families learned who could enroll, what the fees would be, when they would come to camp, when parents could visit, what they would wear, and what else they would need.

Camp Hagan for Girls
"The Camp with a Character"
Shawnee-on-Delaware, Penna.

WHAT TO BRING

A smart two-piece uniform in tan trimmed with brown has been adopted as the official Camp Hagan uniform and is to be worn on all occasions. (See order form.)

I. PERSONAL EQUIPMENT

4 uniforms (as minimun for full season)
3 uniforms (as minimum for two weeks)
2 swimming suits (for season campers)

1 dress	1 halter
1 heavy sweater or jacket	Bathing cap
1 light sweater or jacket	Raincoat or poncho
Riding breeches (for riding only)	Umbrella and rainhat
Anklets	1 laundry bag
Underclothes	Coat hangers
Handkerchiefs	Sewing kit
1 bathrobe	Flashlight
Writing material	Bible

Warm pajamas (pajamas for day wear are not desirable)

II. FOOTWEAR

Bed room slippers	Bathing shoes (Keds preferred)
2 prs. serviceable shoes	Rubbers or galoshes

III. BEDDING EQUIPMENT

4 sheets	4 heavy blankets (one dark one)
2 pillow slips	1 comfortable pillow

IV. TOILET ARTICLES

4 bath towels	Soap, tooth brush
4 wash cloths, mirror	Tooth paste, comb, nail file, etc.

VERY DESIRABLE

Musical instruments	Costumes
Tennis racket and balls	Camera
Scout knife	Scout axe
Colored neckerchiefs	Archery equipment
Poncho	Camp cooking utensils (Sr. girls only)

HAVE YOUR NAME ON ALL YOUR BELONGINGS

Please be sure that every article of your clothing is distinctly marked with your full name. For this purpose, Washproof Name Tapes made by Sterling Name Tape Co., 1322 Station Street, Winsted, Conn., are recommended. The price is 75 cents for 100 and 50 cents for each additional 100, same name, etc. Attach the tape so that your name will be in plain sight when the article is folded in the most natural manner. Have your name or some identifying mark on everything you bring to camp.

What to Bring

Dr. West Tooth Brushes

Old style, with pig bristles, claimed waterproof, 35 cents
New style, Nylon bristles, really waterproof, with glass container, vacuum-cup holder, 50 cents

Prices include postage and engraving owner's name

Name-on Handkerchiefs
Hemstitched Borders

Handkerchiefs with name of owner neatly printed with indelible ink. Saves all the work of sewing on name tapes. Does not add to the cost of handkerchiefs. Postpaid

No. 2 Ladies' size, 11 x 11, first quality cotton handkerchiefs, 90 cents per dozen.

No. 4 Ladies' size, 11 x 11, Irish Linen, $2.20 per dozen.

No. 7 Boys' size, 13 x 13, first quality cotton handkerchiefs, $1.20 per dozen.

Name-on Towels and Wash Cloths

Heavy weight, first quality turkish towels and wash cloths with owner's name indelibly printed on both ends of towels and on one side of wash cloths. Postpaid.

Medium size towels, 18 x 36. No. 12 all white. No. 11 colored borders. 23 cents each. No. 24 colored borders, extra heavy, 35 cents each.

Large size, heavy towels, 22 x 44. No. 15 all white. No. 19 colored borders, 45 cents each.

No. 16. Wash cloths, extra heavy. Colored borders, 10 cents each. No. 30, all white, 10 cents.

Name Tape Boilproof Cement

For attaching name tapes to cloth and other materials and for mending almost everything. 25 cents

Send orders to
Sterling Name Tape Company

Extras

16

Girls from eight to sixteen could enroll and would be divided into Junior (ages 8-12) and Senior (12-16) groups. The fee to send a girl to camp was $10 for Lutherans, $12 for non-Lutherans. Campers were to arrive on Saturdays, brought by their parents, if possible, so that parents could meet the counselors and get an idea of the camp and the program. However, if necessary, girls could be sent by train, to be met at the Delaware Water Gap railroad station, or by bus to the terminal in Stroudsburg.

Visiting days would be Saturdays and Sundays ONLY. Mail should be identified by "bunkhouse" number, a carry-over from Camp Miller, where boys lived in bunkhouses, in turn inherited from the pioneering American West.

All campers would wear the Camp Hagan uniform, a "smart two-piece ensemble in tan, trimmed with brown and monogrammed in white." Price, $2.00. Along with this description, a young woman stands in the new uniform, her blouse tucked in, creases ironed in her shorts, saluting sharply. Two uniforms were suggested for campers staying two weeks, and at least four for those staying longer. A list of other clothing and equipment was included – here we first see the ubiquitous boots and poncho – with the requirement that everything be marked with the owner's name.

C. H. UNIFORM

Uniform 1937

Camp fees were returnable in the event of illness or in disciplinary action deemed best for the camp. The rule, familiar to all Hagan campers, that no food be brought or sent unless there was enough for the whole camp, first appears in the 1937 sales brochure. At first, fruit was excepted. The brochure also told parents and prospective campers about the permanent buildings and equipment at camp, as well as the programs and departments that would provide instructional and entertainment activities, along with food and medical care.

The grounds of play space and wooded areas would provide opportunity for nature study and woodcraft (Pioneering), two of the topics so motivational in the early camping movement around the turn of the century. The 1500 feet of waterfront, it was claimed, would afford "unsurpassable swimming and boating."

The cabins, eight in the Junior Camp and four in the Senior, would be thirty-five feet long and twenty feet wide, each with a flush lavatory, wash basin, and cot beds with five-inch mattresses. Along with closet space, each camper would have two shelves at the back of the cabin – the beloved cubbies – for clothing and towels, and three (very) small shelves by her bed.

Each cabin would have a front porch, painted white. The cabins themselves would be "chocolate" colored, roofed with varicolored shingles. And each would have electricity. This description reflects the hopes and plans of the Ministerium planners – it does not say what was actually there when camp opened for the first summer.

A dining hall, 100 feet by 52 feet, would have modern furnishings and kitchen equipment, a large fireplace, and hardwood floors. (Campers who scrubbed those floors would come to know every foot and board!) There was to be a large airy shower house for each unit. A Dispensary and Infirmary would serve the medical needs of the camp, and an attractive and comfortable Office would house administrative work.

Program and Departments

Descriptions of the programs and departments in the sales brochure reflected the hopes and plans, if not always the actual outcomes, of the camp planners. *Program* is what would go on at camp, and the *departments* were both real places where things went on and, more abstractly, the counselors and department heads who helped the program happen. The departments would be Aquatics, Arts and Crafts, Athletics, Dramatics and Entertainment, Religious Activity, and the two supporting departments, Culinary and Medical.

The **Aquatics Department** counselors were all to be American Red

18

Cross Life Guards supervised by two "American Red Cross Examiners," a level of training by the Red Cross focusing on managing water facilities. In the early years of summer camps (1880 - 1920), well before Camp Hagan, swimming was a key part of the activities, but there was little formal instruction. Campers who could already swim passed swimming, boating, and rescue tests, and there was a lot of jumping off rocks or a diving tower if there was one, and swinging from ropes out into the water. But in that time, those who couldn't swim weren't taught – they just played in the water in shallow safe areas.

In the 1920s, however, summer camps began cooperating with the American Red Cross lifesaving and water safety programs. The Red Cross promoted swimming lessons for everyone, as well as physical changes to make waterfront areas safer.

Camp Hagan's swimming program would be based on two principles: "Every Camper a Swimmer" and "Safety, First, Last, and Always." Though experienced Hagan campers might smile at the rapturous description of the waterfront as "one of the finest beaches along the Delaware River," none would ever fault the serious attention to instruction and safety as well as the investment of caring and hard work on the part of the waterfront staff. Swims, it was hoped, would occur three times daily, with "Tag" and "Buddy" systems ensuring safety. These were not defined, so parents of prospective campers would have to entrust their daughter to the Aquatics staff on faith. And there would be a "fine fleet" of canoes and rowboats.

Arts and Crafts would have three associate directors. One of them, Herman W. Stoldt (Bear Heart), would teach Indian Arts and Crafts and outdoor cooking. Bear Heart was Camp Miller's "Indian Counselor" and would now share his time and knowledge with Camp Hagan. A picture in the sales brochure for 1937 shows Bear Heart in the woods wearing traditional headdress and clothing.

The **Athletic Department** was to be directed by an "experienced Physical Education Instructor." There were expected to be *several* baseball diamonds, a hockey field, and tennis courts. Instruction would be given each day in these and other sports, and all games would be supervised. Athletics would also include "corrective exercises" (posture, for example), "rhythmical" and interpretive dancing" – and fencing!

Dramatics and Entertainment would include both program planning and instruction, to be directed "by an expert program planner." The organizers looked forward to "Talking Motion Pictures, Musical Comedies, Skits, Short Plays, and happy campfire programs."

Bear Heart

There was to be, as well, a Directress of Music who would organize singing and instrumental groups. There would be courses in general dramatics, stage work, and outdoor dramatics and pageants in the Greek amphitheater.

Although nature study and pioneer campcraft were mentioned as a "draw" of the location, the description of departments in the 1937 sales brochure doesn't mention either one.

Finally, in programs and activities for campers, there was to be a **Religious Activity Department**. Each day would have a short Matins and Vespers worship, with Vespers in the outdoor chapel if weather allowed. Visiting pastors were to come to conduct Vespers and Sunday Church service. After Taps there would be "Fireside Chats" with the cabin counselors, "who understand girls' problems."

In the **Culinary Department**, menus would be planned by the Director, Marie Staub, who in her professional health work had specialized in nutrition. Camp Hagan girls would "enjoy the best in foods, deliciously prepared and tastily served," just as at Camp Miller.

20

The **Medical Department** was the other service department foreseen by the camp planners. Ever since summer camping started at the end of the 19th century, health and safety had been important issues, though in the early years not much was known about how to camp and be safe at the same time. With boys digging latrines and then preparing food, sanitation was often not reliable. Water quality was uncertain, and typhoid occurred often. Swimming, particularly, was rife with opportunity for accidents as boys competed to jump off rocks along their lakeside.

But, in fact, the camp Medical Department met campers long before campers met the nurse on campus. Toward the end of the sales brochure parents would find the "Past Medical History and Certificate of Health" which must be done by a licensed physician, no more than one week before camp. Diseases, operations, and vaccinations were to be listed. Since they were dealing with girls here, there was another matter to be noted: had the daughter matured? If not, had she been prepared for it?

And, on the last page of the sales brochure, we find "Suggestions From Parents:" "Do you use any agent to regulate your daughter's bowels? If so, what and how often?" followed by requests for advice from the parents about what foods might disagree with the girl and what restrictions on exercises might be advisable. Finally, there were "Remarks," where parents could list "habits, attitudes, or characteristics" that they wished to be "corrected or instilled." At the very end, in parentheses, parents are urged: "(This report must be carefully filled out. It will be an invaluable guide in the understanding and direction of your daughter.)" So, a girl in 1937 wasn't just forging into the wilderness for recreation and a return to the land. Indeed, she took with her a good bit of baggage, not of her own choosing, besides the suitcase or trunk she toted.

But these requests of parents for information on how to guide their daughters into healthy and attractive womanhood may have been somewhat pro forma. It was the way a camp brochure ought to look. In early years there is no evidence that any counselor or unit head acted on

21

whatever advice, if any, they received. Perhaps there wouldn't be such evidence, if they had. But there is considerable evidence from Year One and forward that many girls loved their time at Hagan. They grew socially, found themselves spiritually deepened, and were well and truly physically fortified.

Later Years

Although at the turn of the 20th century many camps closed after only a few seasons, by the interwar years (the time that Camp Hagan began) the camping industry was booming and Hagan entered a scene of great popularity for summer camps. In this context, and with the Ministerium's enthusiasm for the new camp and their support and attention, the sales brochure for 1937 could justifiably claim "Camp Hagan...will be so complete that you will not believe that it is its first year of operation."

Endnotes

[12] Peter Paul Hagan: Carpet manufacturer, director of James Lees & Sons Co., president of Charles P. Cochrane Co., and chairman of the board of Lees-Cochrane Co. Active in formation of Lutheran Church of America. http://www.findagrave.com/cgi-bin/fg.cgi?page=gr&GRid=51666150.

Chapter 3

The Lay of the Land

Don't know much about geography
Don't know much about geology
adapted from Sam Cooke, "Wonderful World"

Located between a long, not very high mountain and the Delaware River below, Camp Hagan was built on reclaimed farm fields in the Minisink Valley, considered prime bottom land.

Before the farms, there were mixed hardwood forests and the Lenape Native Americans who thrived in them. And before that, there was ice. In the Ice Age, four major glaciers, in turn, made their inexorable way down the North American continent. The last of the four great glaciers is known as the Wisconsin glacier, named for the source of the material gathered up and pushed along and, ultimately, left as the glacier receded for the last time. Sometimes gouging out river valleys and lake beds, sometimes leaving great mounds of rocky debris, the miles-high glaciers carved and molded the hills we know as the Poconos and the Delaware River Valley.

Why does this matter? You'll see.

It may disappoint us to learn that the Poconos are actually a massive plateau, not really mountains. Geologically the southernmost region of the Catskills, the Pocono Plateau on the northwest is part of the Allegheny Plateau, a range of the Appalachian mountain chain. On the Pocono Plateau, Mt. Minsi is a steeply rising mountain on the Pennsylvania side of the Delaware Water Gap, across from Mt. Tammany on the New Jersey side. Of the three tribes of the Lenni (Leni) Lenape people, the Minsi branch lived in the area of what would become Camp Hagan. They had been known as a peaceful tribe, who considered the Minisink their free-ranging territory. The river valley at Minisink

Island was the site of their council seat and council fire.

The Poconos were not so spectacular as the rocky looming ranges to the West, but they had a gentleness, a restfulness, where people could snuggle in the mild folds of the hills, and there Camp Hagan was lodged between the low mountain and the river on the northwestern bank.

Camp Hagan was 3.7 miles north of Camp Miller, 7.7 miles above Shawnee-on-Delaware, and another approximately six miles from the nearby town of Stroudsburg. U. S. Route 209 was the major route on the northwest side, paralleling that stretch of the Delaware. From the

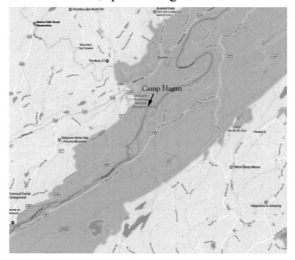

southwest, US Route 611 came in from Scranton and Wilkes Barre, and 209 came from Mauch Chunk and Harrisburg. Route 12 led to Philadelphia, Allentown, or Reading. To the south was the Delaware Water Gap and routes leading from Easton and New York City.

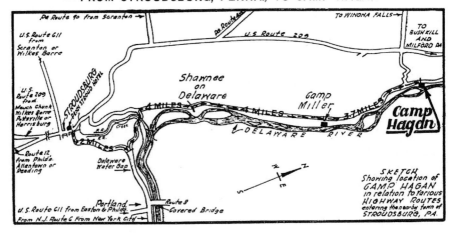

— FROM STROUDSBURG, PENNA., TO CAMP HAGAN —

25

To get to Camp Hagan, you left River Road for the Freeman Tract Road, unpaved and known locally as Lower Hogback Road, which closely followed the river.

Camp Hagan lay about forty feet above the Delaware River. [13] The "mountain," about two miles long, rose about 280 feet above camp to the west. Although campers and local residents called parts of the hill the Hogback and The Roller Coaster, the hill itself did not have a particular name. All campers who have returned to the area agree: the mountain was much higher when we were girls at camp.

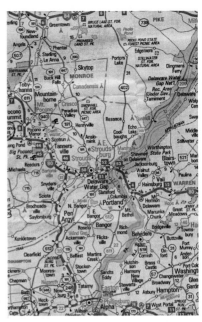

Northeast Pennsylvania

About halfway up the hill, behind camp, was a big chunk of cement, housing a spring and pump for the camp's water known to Haganites as "Hitler's Tomb." According to Esther "Sis" Wenrich, Director of Athletics in the first year, Hitler's Tomb was named by Hagan's first director, Gladys Staub. At that point Hitler had begun the rearmament of Germany, and Nazism was rampant, but the invasion of Poland was not until 1939, so this naming was a curious and very prescient thing to have occurred in the Poconos in 1937.

The River and the Weather

> *That was a tough river. That river was no slouch.*
> Jane Endres Hock

The Delaware begins in the Catskill Mountains in Eastern New York, forming much of the boundary between New York and Pennsylvania, then between Pennsylvania and New Jersey, and heads

26

for the sea at Delaware Bay. The Delaware Water Gap, one of the scenic wonders of the United States, is, of course, the namesake of the Delaware Water Gap National Recreation Area. More on that later, because it is part of the ultimate history of Camp Hagan and all the river camps.

The Delaware is navigable for large ships to Philadelphia and smaller ships to Trenton.[14] Above that the river is relatively shallow, suitable for canoes, rafts, and kayaks. In times of drought, when the river is low, it's a bumpy ride. If the river was high from prolonged rains, some camp events had to be canceled, such as water sports or water pageants. On the other hand, if there was a drought, the river might be too low and canoe trips would have to be postponed. Or there might be a water shortage in camp. And swimming was different from swimming in pools or lakes. In former director Jane Endres Hock's words, "Anyone who learned to swim in the Delaware on the Hagan side [the deep channel] was a strong swimmer."

The Pocono area is in what is known as a *humid subtropical climate zone*,[15] meaning that summers are hot and muggy. There are some places in the world where people say, "If you don't like the weather, just wait an hour, it'll change." But that's not true in the upper Delaware Valley. There, if it's hot, it stays hot for a long time. Even William Penn[16] in 1683, reporting back to the trading company in England, spoke of the "extraordinary heat."

Building Camp Hagan

> *The campus was wide open and bare*
> *except near the river bank and*
> *a tree or two in the Senior Unit.*
> Posie Bocek Clymer

In the 1940s, publications of professional designs for camps and cabins were available, for example in *Park and Recreation Structures*, but that was after Camp Hagan began. In the 1930s and before, camp layout usually was the responsibility of camp directors, and structures were built by local craftsmen, builders, carpenters, and sometimes camp personnel. Camps were normally built of local materials – wood and stone. In the beginning of the 1937 sales brochure we read, "All thru the Winter months, the minds and hands of architects, engineers, contractors, and builders have been busy building for you the new Camp Hagan."

According to a *Building & Repairs* report, based on synod records, the land for Camp Hagan cost $7,125.00, and the tennis courts, "Mess Hall," and twelve cabins $27,060.00. A later note in the report adds: "Costs on all camps (Miller, Ministerium, and Hagan) is unclear. Sometimes the building was done by a contractor but most often the camps bought supplies and had the caretaker build." At the July 4, 1937 dedication of the opening of Camp Hagan, a Mr. Dimick, "with his force of men," is credited with having constructed the buildings for the camp.[17] According to the *Building and Repairs*" report, "more property" was bought for Hagan in 1939, but we don't know how much.

In the beginning years of summer camps, around the turn of the 19th to 20th centuries, campers and counselors slept on open ground in a blanket or bedroll. The next step was tents on the ground. Then came tents on raised platforms, and finally cabins. Even tents on the ground were considered by some early purists as too soft, too easy for real camping. But tents had to be put up and taken down each year, and they were hard to maintain. According to the *Building and Repairs* report, Miller transitioned to cabins from 1927 to 1931, but Hagan's Shanty Town remained to the end.

Although the military-style parade ground and neat rows of tents led to easier control over boisterous campers, private camp owners and organizations that sponsored camps became more interested in creating lovely views of water and natural landscapes that looked good in advertising brochures. At the site of Camp Hagan, the height of the riverbank and trees and undergrowth meant no major water views from most of campus level, and the campus itself, laid out across a long, former farm field, was not yet charming. But in the 1937 sales brochure is a lovely aerial picture taken from the river bank, late sun reflecting on an expanse of water, framed by tree branches in the foreground.

"FOR YOUR BOATING AND SWIMMING"

There were, as planned, twelve cabins, eight Junior, four Senior. The Junior cabins stretched in a gentle curve at the south end of campus, while the four Senior cabins sat at the north end – a somewhat military model, with the open campus like a parade ground but without the straight rows of cabins and squared-off paths in between. Behind the senior unit was the chapel, council fire ring, and the outdoor theater. Each cabin held eight beds, housing seven campers and a counselor. Not all cabins were full this first year, particularly in the senior unit. For later campers, this much space would have been an unknown luxury.

At the center of the campus was the Administration Building, first called "The Office" in the 1937 sales brochure and then "Headquarters" in the daily newssheet *The Queue*, and later, permanently, the "Rat Trap."

Great Hall, called the Dining Hall in the sales brochure and the Mess Hall in the *Buildings and Repairs* report, but already "Great Hall" in the 1937 summer *Queue* and on the building itself, was located to the front and left of the Administration Building (if you were facing the river). Great Hall

29

played a large role in camp life because, besides providing space for three meals a day, it was the only place big enough to hold the whole camp for entertainments and gatherings. Early senior campers remember moving the big square tables and folding chairs out onto the back porch when space was needed, and then back in again for the next meal. A big stone fireplace anchored Great Hall at the kitchen end of the building, used when seniors had unit meetings. There was also a piano, an upright donated by Fred Koehler of Bethlehem, husband of the camp cook. The kitchen was attached to Great Hall but not accessible to campers or staff, except at the serving windows.

The only other building at this time was the Infirmary-Dispensary, to the back and right of the Administration Building, close to the river bank. According to the 1937 Sales brochure, there were both Junior and Senior Shower Houses. The *Building & Repairs* report says Hagan showers were installed in 1939 (at a cost of $878), but Director Sis (Esther) Wenrich says the shower houses were available the first year.

So, over many hundreds of years, the grounds on which Camp Hagan was built went from wilderness to farm land and back to a sort of wilderness, now a designed and controlled one, where girls could experience nature safely while learning to live, work, and play together.

Endnotes

[13] Information gathered by Chris Hill Killough at the Delaware Water Gap National Recreation area, 2011. Also Jane Grigger, personal communication, 2011

[14] Encarta Encyclopedia, http://www.delawareriver.net/history/php, 4/22/2011

[15] from Wikipedia, http://en.wikipedia.org/wiki/Philadephia, 10/31/2010

[16] Shukaitus, p. 154

[17] *Building and Repairs*

Chapter 4

The First Years – 1937-1939

From the mountains here at Hagan,
To the river down below
We have come to spend the summer's happy hours.
(To the tune of *The Whiffenpoof Song*)

In 1937, just north of Shawnee-on-Delaware in the Pennsylvania Poconos, Camp Hagan opened its first season. It would last for thirty-four years, and many thousands of girls would sleep in its cabins, eat in Great Hall, and swim at its waterfront.

Cabin 1937

On that first Saturday, July 3, more than eighty girls arrived, some by car, some by train into Stroudsburg to be picked up by the camp truck. After being greeted by the director and the camp nurse in their dress whites, the girls received their cabin assignments. Then they trundled their suitcases and trunks by wheelbarrow to their cabins. Most were looking forward to this adventure. But we can imagine the uncertainty and, for some, a little anxiety. Long later, we can appreciate the invention, creativity, and experimentation that went into this day and all the rest to come.

Besides basic buildings (Ch. 3), there were baseball diamonds, a hockey field, tennis courts (ah, the tennis courts: this will be an ongoing theme), outdoor chapel, volleyball courts, an archery range, horseback riding trails, and a shuffleboard court. In 1939 a new infirmary with a shaded back porch overlooking the river would appear. Trees had indeed been planted – maybe not the promised hundreds, but many.

Echoing the nostalgia for pioneer abilities and practices emphasized in early 20th century camping, the daily news sheet, *The Queue*, in its first issue, announced: THE STAFF OF THE QUEUE WELCOMES YOU – PIONEERS on "the very first day for Camp Hagan – and more important, you are its very first campers." [Signed] Dusty (Director Marie Staub).

The Camp Hagan dedication service was held the next day, on Sunday, July 4, 1937. Mr. and Mrs. Peter Paul Hagan, who had donated the land, were there to see the results of their generosity and receive the thanks of grateful Hagan girls and women. The Hagans also came on a Saturday later in the summer to visit. Lutherans in the area were proud of this addition to the camping program. Early in the summer Hagan welcomed the "ladies from the Lutheran churches of Stroudsburg" for a visit.

The Daily Schedule

Schedules organize people's lives. Understanding the schedule and changes will help us understand the beginnings of Camp Hagan. We might want to know, for example, how much time is allowed for waking up, for dressing? For eating? A half hour per meal for 100 or so girls may be very short. For a church-sponsored camp, how is religion reflected in the times allotted for formal religious practices? And finally, the daily schedule matters because the way children are moved through their day – leisurely? fast? – affects the way children grow and the way they feel about their camp day.

Later campers will recognize in these first years many familiar daily events that remained much the same over the years. How did the

33

schedule come to be?

Early camps, around the turn of the 20th Century, well before Camp Hagan appeared on the scene, did not have much formal scheduling. There was always work to do since one of the early principles had been to have campers, rather than staff, do everything, as pioneers would have done on the westward trail. There might be a few scheduled activities like sports or swimming, but otherwise the day evolved according to camper and counselor interests and weather.

Soon, in line with rigid scheduling in the public workplace and in schools, camp schedules came to be very tightly controlled. The days were chock-full of five- and ten-minute segments. The 1910s and early '20s saw the peak of the highly structured camp model. By the 1920s, most camps had careful hour-by-hour planning, with an emphasis on competitive sports, and awards to winners in sports and to best behaved campers. At large boys' camps, campers were divided into increasing numbers of "tribes," who moved from one activity to another to the sound of bugles or bells, combining American Indian and military models.[18]

In the years before Hagan opened, camps had come under criticism for overscheduling. Camp Hagan's schedule itself was pretty tightly organized, with activities on the hour, the half hour, sometimes even shorter segments, like camps of the previous decade.

First Schedule

The Daily Schedule in the sales brochure for 1937 manages to get Reveille, Calisthenics ("Setting Up Exercises"), Optional Morning Dip – get into bathing suits, down to the waterfront, swim, climb up from the waterfront, and out of suits – Flag Raising, and Matins all in an hour. Finally, breakfast at 8.00!

The order of Flag Raising at 7:45 and Matins at 7:50 suggests that the Matins service was held with the camp as a group in front of Great Hall just before breakfast. One camper, Norie McIlvaine Clague, remembers from the first year "morning Matins around the flagpole." However, others of our earliest campers swear it never happened that way. "Matins in the morning in the cabin," says another early camper, Posie Bocek Clymer.

Calisthenics and Optional Morning Dip were gone by 1939, making for a much less pressed beginning of the day, but Flag Raising at 7:45 and Matins at 7:50 remained in the sales brochures until 1941.

Activities and instruction in athletics, riding, swimming, arts and crafts, and nature and pioneering filled the hours after morning Kapers (cabin chores) at 8:30 and after Rest Period, 1:00 to 2:00. Though 1937 saw inspection following Rest Period, in the next few years Inspection does not appear in the schedule at all. It was moved to the beginning of morning instruction periods in the 1940s, where it made more sense, with campers out of the cabins and Kapers freshly done. In 1939 Canteen was spliced in at 2:10, and this would last for a few years.

After supper, Campus Games and Athletics, Vespers, Evening Program, Cabin Devotions, and Taps at 9:15 PM made up the rest of the day. In 1937, "Retreat (Flag Lowering) *and* Vespers" were scheduled at 6:00, with Canteen again at 6:10, allowing apparently only ten minutes for those two events. However, in 1939 Vespers was moved to 7:30 for twenty minutes, after Retreat, Canteen, and Campus Games.

By 1939 the Daily Schedule allows ten minutes for Cabin Devotions, no longer called Squad Devotions. The switch from words like *mess* to Dining Hall (later Great Hall), *squad* to cabin mates, and *bunk* to cabin, signals the fading of the military theme inherited from early 20th century camping. Indian and pioneer motifs remained strong.

Early Camp Life

Little is known about **counselors** in these early years, other than staff lists kept in the *Wooden Album* (See Headwaters). It is known that they had days off, and in 1937 "Lu" (Lucille S. Maberry, Athletics) and Tay (then Director for Religious Activity), according to *The Queue*, went to "the Big City" (presumably New York) and reported "a swell time." And we have a list of Hagan's first staff (App. 2) as well as a photo.

The ratio of counselors to campers was one to seven at the start, then by 1939, one to eight. Campers and counselors in later years, when there were eleven or so campers to one counselor, even counting unit heads and department heads, may envy that earlier average

Camp pictures began immediately. The first known picture, shown below, was taken July 30th, at the end of the first month.

Meals were taken in Great Hall, with only half an hour allowed for each, and there was singing after meals. On supper hikes the first campers took bag lunches – sandwich, fruit, perhaps a cookie. Actually, that's what later campers took, too. There was a "progressive supper," when Seniors served the main course, Juniors the beverages, and Intermediates "the surprise course of the evening" – dessert – and also a "nosebag supper," a bag lunch that cabin groups could take to eat anywhere on campus.

One food item keeps reappearing in *The Queue* – "Howard's buns." These were a favorite breakfast treat. The only complaint seemed to be that there weren't enough of them because they were so good. And A. G. (Alice G.) Finley, Director of Nature Study, kept fresh flowers on the tables in Great Hall. How pretty that must have been. That didn't carry over into the following years, though.

What's Going On?

In the 1937 sales brochure, departments were arranged by number of staff. The Aquatic Program had five, the Athletic Department – four, Arts and Crafts – three, plus Chief Bearheart, whose generous services were shared with Camp Miller, Dramatics and Entertainment – two, Pioneering and Nature and Religious Activity – one each.

Aquatics

At the turn of the 20th century swimming was seen almost entirely as recreation. In fact, it was generally called bathing (think *bathing* suit). At early boys' camps, boys who couldn't swim were given a safely roped off "crib" but didn't receive instruction. Things were very different at Camp Hagan from the beginning. Swimming was another means to physically fortify campers, and by then the general approach to swimming had changed.

The two principles for the waterfront – "Safety First" and "Every Girl a Swimmer" – were put into action by "Skipper" (Kathryn Reinbold), Head Swimming Counselor.

Safety First

Down on the waterfront there were ropes, anchored at the shore, with rowboats spaced along the lines and small white floats between them. Two counselors stood in each boat, watching the swimmers play, alert to any problem. Holding onto the ropes was off-limits. If a girl slipped under the ropes, she would be at the mercy of the strong current. Because the river had a fairly swift drop-off on the Hagan side of the Delaware, campers were

The first waterfront

generally careful and the waterfront counselors, eagle-eyed.

Campers participated in their own safety by way of the buddy system, which required that girls go into the water with a partner, and when the waterfront head blew the whistle, all pairs would hold up their clasped hands. A partner-less swimmer spelled trouble. The tag board was another safety check. Girls brought their swim tags from a board at the top of the steps down to the waterfront and placed them on a corresponding board there. When girls had returned to their cabins, any tag left down below warranted sending someone to verify her presence on land. In later years, the name of the forgetful girl was broadcast over the loudspeaker, with orders to appear at the Rat Trap immediately.

Every Girl a Swimmer

The swim cap colors designated swimmers' ability levels – not quite the same as those that later campers would recognize. The Red Cap was for Beginners, but this was the beginners' class, unlike later years where campers had to pass the beginners' test to be *in* the beginners' class. In *The Queue* in this first year there is much urging of seniors, especially, to "get out of the Beginner's class."

> *Congratulations Senior girls, Lois Holman and Margaret*
> *Graver* [poss. Graber], *for passing your green cap tests.*
> *Come on Red Caps. Dot Ross and Dorothea Hasskarl have*
> *passed the tests for Jr. Life Saving. We're proud of you, too.*

The Queue expressed appreciation for the waterfront staff: "What satisfaction it must give to see a camper advance from red cap to green to blue and then become a Junior Life Saver." And the cap color for Junior Life Savers? *The Queue* asks: "How many more white caps will there be?" and of the largest Life Saving class of the summer: "Won't a few more white caps look good on our waterfront?" White cap, which later designated those with little or no water experience, was, in 1937, the cap color for those who had passed Junior Life Saving.

Girls swam twice a day, with mornings devoted to instruction, afternoons to free swim. After swimming, campers hung their suits out on the lines in back of the cabins to dry, sort of. With two swims a day plus nighttime dew, there wasn't much drying time. In the first year, Zipper (V. Elizabeth) Cameron, Director of Pioneer Camping, and her Pioneers put up the posts in back of the cabins for the clotheslines.

"Juniors – try to pass your blue cap test so that you, too, may ride in

'Josie' Pittinger's little green boat," urges *The Queue*. We don't know anything more about the little green boat, but it must have been fun. Canoeing and boating were so popular that Skipper had to divide classes. Juniors and Intermediates came from 11-12 in the morning, Seniors 7 to 7:30 in the evening. The Boating and Canoeing Club went for a moonlight ride.

Camp Hagan's love affair with canoe trips began early. Notices in *The Queue* of 1937 focus more on funny accidents than on the romance of the river. At Sandy Beach, somebody lost her shoes. On another canoe trip, the packers forgot forks and spoons and had to eat their beans out of cups. We will hear more about canoe trips in coming chapters – the idea was never far from campers' hearts.

The 1937 *Queue* reports that "Mac, Kitty Lu and Pat" [Ruth McLaughlin, Katherine L. Reuman; "Pat" unknown] swam across the river and back just for the exercise.

The Aquatics Department sometimes provided entertainment. On a Sunday in August 1937 there was to have been a Water Pageant. However, due to a previous week of rain, the river was still high, and the Water Pageant was postponed. Instead, there would be a Water Carnival that afternoon, up on the campus. How the water part was accomplished is unknown.

Athletics

Besides attending their assigned swim times, girls went around to the other departments for activities throughout the day. From the beginning, Athletics was one of the main departments at Camp Hagan (Ch. 2), led by Sis Wenrich.

About the tennis courts – In 1939, backstops were installed. The writer of the 1939 sales brochure proclaimed, "No more chasing the balls in the tall grass!" Can you imagine playing tennis with no backstop?

In these first years there was a busy tournament life. The "series opener" of the softball tournament took place in the first week of camp. The Daily Schedule listed "6:30-7:50 P.M., Campus Games/Athletics."

This hour and twenty minutes was largely filled with baseball according to *The Queue*, although our earliest camper/counselors say it was always softball. Counselors played the Senior Girls, Intermediates challenged the winner, Counselors beat the Intermediates, Intermediates challenged the Seniors, Juniors lost to the Intermediates, an exhibition game between Senior 1 and 2 vs Senior 3 and 4 was held, and the Seniors beat all of the counselors and campers together. And then there were rematches.

These games went on for days, since only three or four innings could be played at a time. We may suspect all this baseball frenzy had something to do with the athletic counselors' own favorite sport. After all, baseball *was* the national pastime.

Other sports included tennis, volley ball, shuffleboard, and occasional calisthenics and posture exercises. Henrietta Miller, Senior 4, won a jacks tournament. Three points to note here: First, this emphasis on competitive sports between cabin or unit groups and counselors, with the rest of the camp as spectators, reflected a practice of very early 20th century summer camps, forty years before Camp Hagan. Second, calisthenics and setting-up exercises also recall an earlier time in camping history when military-style activities were more in vogue. And third, the enjoyment of competitive sports carried external American culture in the early part of the 20th century into the camp scene.

On Friday at the end of the third two-week session, a bale of straw appeared, piled high on the porch of Headquarters. The next day, "Robin Hoods" from Camp Miller came to Hagan to give an archery exhibition. On Monday of the seventh week, Sis, head of Athletics, was to begin her classes "in the ancient art." *The Queue* reported the first bull's eye by Ben Walker, known as the Babe Didrikson of Camp Hagan.

Young archers 1939

Horseback Riding

Many later campers never knew that Camp Hagan in its first years had horseback riding, using horses from a nearby farm. On Monday morning of the second week of camp, 1937, the first group of riders left camp at 8:30 led by counselor A. G. Finley. By the second month of the season, so many girls wanted to participate that riding was limited to season campers. For those campers who were able to take part in horseback riding activities, it was great fun, especially putting on horse shows. Riding expanded the Athletics Department's contribution to the "Physically Fortify" goal.

Arts and Crafts

The Arts and Crafts building was simply called the Craft Shop, but we don't know where the first campers actually did their craft work – the Lutheran *Minutes* tell us that the first Arts and Crafts Building was built in 1941. *The Queue* kept campers posted about Arts and Crafts doings. One week there were special activities in reed, leather, and woodwork, in another week pewter dishes. A loom for weaving pocketbooks was kept in Headquarters. Director of Arts and Crafts "Sunny" (Anne K.) Minnich planned exhibits of campers' craft work, and there was as well an exhibit of professional photography in Headquarters. Sunny praised the girls for good cleaning up after craft activities. Unfortunately, because pencils kept going missing, by the second half of the summer campers would have to bring their own pencils or face an unspecified penalty.

Camp Miller Arts and Crafts sent an exhibit of masks and wood-carvings by counselors (displayed in Headquarters, either for safety from curious little hands or because the Arts and Crafts area did not yet have the space for such exhibits) and an exhibit of water colors by a counselor in Miller's Art Department. Sunny, in turn, organized craft exhibits by Hagan campers and staff to be sent to Miller.

Arts and Crafts, integrally involved in other parts of camp life, provided decorations for various special events. For Hagan Christmas, campers were urged to get materials from the Craft Shop to make their gifts and Christmas decorations.

There were also clubs in various departments that campers could join, sometimes through competitive audition. The Art and Crafts club was called "H.P.A." The meaning of the letters was not disclosed. *The Queue* announced in 1937 that the H.P.A. would have tryouts, to which campers were to bring their best talents along with pencil, paper, and eraser. H.P.A. announced three new members and promised, "For the losers" there would be another tryout. This time all candidates would be accepted. Perhaps the competitive nature with which this club started out gave way to a more inclusive goal for more members in order for there to be enough members at all. The H.P.A. went on a supper hike, displayed art work in *The Queue,* and described themselves as "always ready with pencil and paper."

Besides the H.P.A. Club, the "Owls" were another club, the purpose of which we'll never know. There was also a "G.A." society, also unexplained. It is likely that these "clubs" were not as exclusive as they might sound, but more probably simply a way to get a nucleus of girls involved in particular projects within a department.

Entertainment

As American summer camps developed into an industry, entertainment would play an important part in recruiting campers. Generally, entertainments at Camp Hagan were participatory. There were talent shows, sometimes called "Stunt Nights." Paper was a popular prop, as in the Paper Fashion Show. In the first year, each cabin dressed two people and brought them to Great Hall to compete with other cabins. Campers were asked to bring blankets for Costume Night. Pantomimes were popular in the late '30s, along with charades and impersonations. One night, campers had to act out nursery rhymes, another night to present one song in pantomime. For another entertainment, each cabin came ready to give an impersonation of a world-famous person.

Treasure hunts and scavenger hunts ensured the participation of all campers. Cabin groups taught songs to the rest of the camp or put together songs for a Hagan medley. Birthday Party night, where each person came dressed to picture her birth-month, had prizes for the best costumes. Tay (Director Jane Taylor) does not mention movies in 1938 in her journal, but 1939 had "moving pictures." And in that year a hay ride to Bushkill was a big thrill for Intermediates.

Participatory entertainments implicitly taught cooperation and provided opportunities for leadership and for learning by observing "natural" leaders. Mild competition was built into many of the entertainments – winners of scavenger hunts, treasure hunts, paper fashion parties, pantomimes, or song nights were announced in *The Queue*. It was a gentle, cheerful sort of competition – no ongoing scores were kept.

Movies, on the other hand, were pure spectatorship. *The Queue* shows that in the first year, campers saw movies almost every Thursday night.

"College Hero" was the very first movie shown at Camp Hagan, made in 1927, with a cast that most readers have never heard of. There were cowboys-and-Indians movies and two that promised "a handsome hero."

The showpiece of the 1937 summer was perhaps Shirley Temple and Bill ("Bojangles") Robinson in *The Littlest Rebel* (from 1935). In this film, Shirley Temple's father, a rebel officer, sneaks back to his rundown plantation to see his family and is arrested; a Yankee takes pity and arranges an escape; everyone is captured and the officers are to be executed, but Shirley and Bojangles beg President Lincoln to intervene. Honest!

Some camping authorities, according to social historian Leslie Paris, were against "spectatoritis," feeling that movies typified the perils of modernity.[19] However, in response to the enthusiasm for movies among girls and boys at some camps in New England, counselors began taking campers into a nearby village or town to see movies.[20] This was controversial among camp leaders: it was not authentic camping. But it pleased the campers, and thus was a good sell.

Presenting movies, though, could backfire. Apparently one early cowboys-and-Indians movie at Hagan was so gory, they had to stop in the middle and take the juniors back to their cabins before the older girls finished watching.

Besides movies, there were more traditional kinds of camp presentations in Great Hall. One evening, "Lu" (Kitty Lu Reumann) taught songs. *The Queue* announced the upcoming counselors' show, called "Why Teachers Go Nuts." Campers were advised: "No stamping of feet allowed and please leave John Jacob Jingleheimer Schmidt (an increasingly loud song and a great favorite) in your cabin." Camp Miller gave three entertainments, an evening of "song and fun," a band concert, and a play called *In Aunt Mahaly's Cabin*. This play was first produced in 1925, with the full title of *In Aunt Mahaly's Cabin: A Negro Melodrama in One Act*." The playwright, Paul Green, won the Pulitzer Prize for it in 1927. A synopsis appears in the Cornell Alumni News (Paul Green was a graduate):

45

The 'ha'nts,' always a terrible bugaboo to the superstitious negro, run riot, along with crime and murder and goblins and witches, all to the accompaniment of rolling thunder and flashes of lightning.[21]

Racially, Camps Hagan and Miller had a long way to go. But they were not alone – the same could be said of the rest of the country. In the late '30s such sentiments would not strike most white middle class girls or boys as odd.

The Dramatics Department put on a musical, "Heart of the Rose," with Terrible Aphis terrorizing the Ladybug kingdom. And there were guest entertainers: A German singer gave a voice demonstration one afternoon, "Rev. Harry" provided lollipop treats, and "Uncle Earl and Aunt Jane" showed pictures of India.

Presentations by the Dramatics Department continued in 1938 and 1939. The first in 1938 was "International Night," written by Italia, with "characters and plot by Dramatic class groups, dances by Candy, music by Louise." The stage at one end of Great Hall was set as a ship – the S. S. Hagan. During the rest of the summer the camp enjoyed "Peer Gynt Suite," "The Bishop's Candlesticks," and "Mother Goose's Children."

In 1939 the camp saw "Around the world with the Hagan dancers." Tay pronounced the program "lovely" and said, "our dance department deserves lots of praise." Also in 1939, "Mulligan's Magic," an operetta, "won the hearts of all." (There were fewer of these presentations mentioned in 1939, but Tay's notes for 1939 are generally shorter, and we don't know that more didn't occur.) In these early years we see that the Dramatics Department often had two or even three dedicated counselor positions, and dance and "serious" music were more prominent than in later years.

Religion

Religion had a large part in the life of a camper, like it or not: matins in the morning in the cabin, vespers every evening and prayers

46

at bedtime. That is where I learned to pray aloud by saying sentence prayers.
Posie Bosek Clymer

Religious Activities were part of Camp Hagan's mission to spiritually deepen. The days were bookended by brief religious observances – morning Matins and bedtime Squad Devotions – with a short Vespers Service in the outdoor chapel, conducted by the week's visiting pastor. On Sunday mornings, Lutheran church services were held in Great Hall.

The Queue announced each week who the visiting pastor would be and thanked him at the end. All girls who were confirmed members of "a Church" could take communion. Campers were reminded in *The Queue* to "bring our Bibles with us to services and by our participation make the brief devotionals a real part of our life at Camp Hagan." And the devotionals *were* brief. The Daily Schedule in the 1937 sales brochure allotted ten minutes for Matins, ten minutes for Retreat (Flag Lowering) *and* Vespers, and ten minutes to Squad Devotions. Of course, this schedule was merely a prediction made in time to publish the sales brochure for the first season, and it may have changed before camp ever opened.

In the coming years, we will see changes in the schedule for Religion. One thing never changed: the synod always kept track of how many Lutheran campers were enrolled, relative to campers of other denominations. For the 1936 season at Camp Miller, the Committee on Youth Activities notes, "Fifty-six per cent of the boys attending camp were Lutherans." In 1938 they mention the "constant increase of Lutheran campers at both camps."

In the early years, Sunday evenings were usually given over to events called "Campers' Own," when various cabins or units would put on pageants or other enactments of Bible stories or religious themes, thus combining Religious Activity with Entertainment. These productions were a good example of counselors and younger campers working closely together and provide evidence for the theory that youngsters

47

could do more with the guidance of older participants or guides than on their own, even if the guides were just slightly older (many counselors were not out of their teens).[22]

Pioneering and Nature Study

The Queue announced, in the second week of camp, that Pioneering would "soon have their class in a tent." Zipper, head of Pioneer Camping, said there would be an exhibition of work done by the Pioneer group, similar to the clubs in Arts and Crafts, Aquatics, and other departments. Pioneering was perhaps most notably exemplified by hiking. In fact, around the turn of the 20th century, camping and hikes were nearly synonymous. However, at the turn of the next century, with camps devoted to computers, soccer, and other specialties, the camp-hike link may have been severed.

At the earliest camps, around the turn of the 19th to 20th centuries, campers sometimes arrived at a bus or train terminal and then hiked in to the campsite, carrying their belongings, sometimes for a few miles.[23] Now *that*'s a hike! By the end of the Interwar years, when Camp Hagan was launched, hikes were for pleasure or program purposes, and campers left camp and returned there, on day hikes, supper hikes, or overnight hikes. All counselors were encouraged to take their cabin groups on supper hikes and other day hikes. Department heads or counselors might take girls on a hike specific to their specialty. In 1937 the Arts and Crafts club, H.P.A., went on supper hikes and sketching hikes. On a "novelty" hike, which seems to have been a nature hike, a variety of stones and flowers were collected. Norie McIlvaine got the highest score, with Jane Detweiler ('60s camper Molly LeVan's mother) a close second. A. G., head of Nature Study as well as Pioneering, took the Nature Club on a hike to the top of the mountain above Hitler's Tomb. Sunny (Arts and Crafts) took seniors on a sketching hike.

On one day there were three trips for seniors: ten campers hiked to Bushkill, seven went on a canoe trip, and the H.P.A. Sketchers' club hiked to some unidentified destination. Another day, thirty or more walked to Bushkill Falls by way of the Hogback, while others went to Winona Falls. One Wednesday in August was announced in *The Queue* simply as "Hike day. Sign up." On a hike to Winona Falls, ten miles, seniors got a lift along the way from the visiting pastor. Intermediates generally went the four miles over the Hogback to Bushkill. On yet another day, camper Emily Frantz's father provided hot dogs for a supper hike.

One hike, possibly including the whole camp, went three miles upriver to a sandy beach. Supper was pronounced "swell." A worship service was held on the shore. The camp sang the *Doxology* and walked home in the moonlight. On another hike for the whole camp, campers ate supper at a picnic grove along the river, and each cabin group presented a charade. A hike to Cedar Beach was a highlight of 1938. Hikers had supper, Vespers under the trees, and a walk home by bright starlight.

Of course, now and then it rained. A hike to Bushkill Falls in the rain ended with a rainbow. Hikers to Winona Falls didn't see the Falls because of the rain and came home on the camp truck, which *The Queue* termed "a thrill in itself, to warm soup, a hot bath and bed." You might wonder: a *hot bath*? There were no baths, only showers, and they weren't always hot, but all were home safe. After rainy hikes, campers hung wet clothes on the rafters.

Thus the Daily Schedule outlined both the rituals, such as Flag Raising or Taps, and also the times available for instruction and activities in the departments. What else went on in the first years at Camp Hagan? Special Days, Change and Visitor days, the beloved campfires, and singing! Always singing. All of these helped to build camp culture and cabin life, and through these, enduring traditions.

Endnotes

[18] Paris p. 232
[19] p. 336
[20] Paris, p. 178
[21] *Cornell Alumni News* Ithaca NY, May 17, 1918
https://ecommons.cornell.edu/bitstream/handle/1813/26884/030_32.pdf
?sequence=1&isAllowed=y
[22] For those interested in education theory, this observation references the 20th century dispute between Piaget's theory of stages of individual growth and Vygotsky's work on development in a social environment.
[23] Van Slyck p. 7

Chapter 5

Making Traditions

Everybody take your hats off to Hagan!
Stars of evening shining
Stay on the right side of Camp Hagan
For this is the song we sing.
Hagan Songbook

Hurray! Camp Hagan's first year was a rousing success. The years of 1937-1939 saw the establishment of the traditions so many alums remember from later years.

Change Days and Visiting Days

In the first year, campers could stay for as little as one week or any number of weeks. Administratively it must have been a zoo, with campers arriving and leaving every Saturday and visitors every weekend. A nice provision was that girls without visitors could meet at Headquarters for a hike. One girl, *The Queue* reported, had seventeen visitors. By 1939 the strong recommendation was made that campers stay for two-week sessions. At first only a suggestion, this became the standard model for many years forward. Visiting days of Saturday and Sunday were strictly adhered to, although there were some special events that parents and families were invited to, for example Circus Day and Water Pageant.

Special Days

Special Days involved the whole camp. In the first year, we know of only a few. The Fourth of July, on Sunday in 1937, featured a parade, and prizes were announced the next day in *The Queue*.

There was a Backwards Day on the first Friday of August, before which *The Queue* warned "new" counselors, that is, campers switched to counselor roles, "as to how the new campers" (counselors in real life) would behave: "They will cause much trouble, we are sure." Backwards Day began after rest period. It was not just a camper/counselor switch, but really backwards: Campfire, then swim, putting suits on backwards. Then breakfast. It lasted just through the afternoon; Vespers and entertainment stayed the same. The next day *The Queue* admonished: "The woodpile [Sis says, for campfires] was skipped – gum chewed and rules generally broken. Now that it is over let's get down to our everyday selves."

May Day began in the first year at Hagan. An ancient Northern European celebration, it comes to us as a re-imagined custom from old England, when the girls of the village sang and danced around the maypole in the spring. It's older than Indian or pioneer or military themes and reflects a "back to nature" sentiment prevalent in the early 20th century.

The last Friday in July, the end of the very first month-long session, was chosen for May Day by the staff at the beginning of that week. Although Camp Hagan got off to a flying start, with many plans already in place, there they were, deciding when May Day would be, five days before the event. And, of course, many operations must have worked that way, as the staff and campers felt their way through that first year. Campers were to bring their ballots for May Queen and court to Great Hall at supper, according to *The Queue*. May Day continued on that day until the mid-'60s.

The Queen and her court were to be announced Friday at breakfast with coronation festivities to come in the afternoon. Intermediates would do acrobatics and there would be May Day songs. All were hoping for a "sunshiny warm day."

On Friday, *The Queue* proclaimed:

Hear ye! Hear ye! Subjects of Hagan Kingdom, you are hereby summoned to the coronation of her majesty "Texas" with Lady

Jane attending her. The royal throne will be placed beneath the tall tree. Subjects from far and near in her kingdom will be present to mark this magnificent occasion. Three cheers for our queen and her court.

The Queen wore a pale blue taffeta gown with a white net train, and court ladies wore gowns of green and yellow trimmed with leaves and chains of yellow daisies. (Somehow there was a wardrobe closet!) Jesters entertained with stunts, dances, and songs. And so was born one of the favorite Special Days for Hagan campers throughout the next decades.

First May Queen

***

Below, entertainment for
May Court 1937

The third Friday in July 1938 saw the first **Miller-Hagan dance** for the seniors. Great Hall was decorated as a cabaret, with lighted candles, fresh flowers, and a refreshment table like, in Tay's words, "a white sail boat on a lovely blue sea." The girls had dance cards. On the third Friday of August the dance was at Camp Miller, the Miller Masquerade. The dances in 1939 were also on the third Friday of July and August, one with a barn dance theme with, according to Director Tay, "square dancing and reels, farmers and farmerettes." Says Tay, "Everyone voted it the best dance ever."

The most special Special Day was **Hagan Christmas**. Christmas Eve was held on a Tuesday and Christmas Day was Wednesday in 1937, Wednesday and Thursday in 1938, and in 1939 Thursday and Friday. Notes appeared in the 1937 *Queue*: "12 more days till Xmas." "Do your shopping early. Only 11 more days until Christmas." "Six more days until Xmas." "Two days more." If campers hadn't made their Christmas gifts already, they were urged to see Sunny or Pete (Elinor M. Peterson) in Arts and Crafts about "Spongex animals, pipe cleaner trinkets, woolen or felt objects" of their own design.

In the afternoon of Christmas Eve Day in 1937, senior girls had a popcorn party in Great Hall, making chains of colored rings and popcorn for the counselors to trim the big tree that night. In the evening, the traditions of a bayberry candle lit by the youngest camper and the Yule log burning in the big stone fireplace began. In 1937 the camp saw a play, Dickens' *A Christmas Carol*, in '38 *The Birds' Christmas Carol*, and in '39 *The Legend of the Juggler*.[24] All three emphasized giving as a way to happiness. Girls were told to bring clean socks to hang, with hopes they'd find more than coal on Christmas morning. *The Queue* reports: "The little lights in the cabins looked so pretty when we went from Great Hall to bed and the singing of carols was a beautiful ending to a grand day."

Christmas Day, Wednesday 1937, was a play day, with various contests and activities. In 1938 there was again a play day that Tay felt "worked so well," giving us a sense of the pressure on a director: Did it work? Was it fun?

The first Camp Hagan Christmas banquet was held amid lighted tapers and evergreen boughs. In 1938 the menu featured creamed turkey, and Tay writes that the "second plaque" – a wooden acorn with staff signatures woodburned on it – was hung and awards presented. "Moving pictures" and a play, *Peace Be Unto You*, Tay writes, "ended a glorious day long to be remembered." The program in 1939 again included moving pictures and a pageant on a Christmas story, *Why the Chimes Rang*. And balloons came down from the ceiling.

What Kept the Train on the Tracks?

Rules and awards were integrally involved in keeping many girls – a hundred or so that first year – happy and safe. It may seem strange to talk of rules and awards in the same space. "Rules" suggest Do's and Don'ts, discipline, behavior correction. "Awards" invoke pleasure, accomplishment, and praise. However, from another perspective, many rules were designed to keep campers safe and camp orderly. And, along with fostering pride in accomplishment, awards were designed to encourage campers to behave in ways that would help assure safety and order, and to exemplify for campers the desired traits of cooperation, leadership, good sportsmanship, and kindness to one another. All these attributes and behaviors contributed to camp culture and camp spirit.

Rules

It seems these were incorporated
rather seamlessly into camp life.
Phyllis Kaspareit Davidson

Occasionally *The Queue* urged girls to be on time, answering the bugle calls. There is a reminder to enter and leave Vesper Service in an orderly manner, and a plea to take care of the hymnals, as they were old to start with. But aside from the list of rules in the promotional brochure and whatever was emphasized in announcements at breakfast, we don't

55

find much about rules. This suggests that the camp day was not rule-laden, and also that things must have been working pretty well in these first seasons.

Only two formal, printed rules appear in the 1937 promotional brochure: all campers had to wear the new uniform (that "smart two-piece ensemble"), although with brown monograms, not white, and by 1939 the saluting camper was gone. Second, NO FOOD was to be brought into camp unless there was enough for everyone. Fruit was the exception, and that only lasted the first year, abandoned due to the risk of drawing insects, mice, or worse. Another rule appears at the end of the Daily Schedule: "9:15 P. M. Taps (all quiet)." Early camper Bep Berger recalls other unwritten rules:

> When we went to Vespers:
> no talking after we passed the cross.
> Follow the Kaper chart in your cabin.
> Buddy system in swimming.
> Waiting on tables.

The beginning of the Letter Home tradition (rule) began in the third week of camp in the first year, when *The Queue* says:

> It seems that some of us have forgotten the folks at home and therefore on Tuesday when we report for supper, admittance to Great Hall will depend upon whether or not we bring an unsealed letter addressed to them.

Besides assuring parents that their daughters still existed, the letters home sometimes filled an advertising function as well, as when *The Queue* urged "Don't forget to tell them about the Camp Hagan Water carnival...help us to get a good audience." In later years, when the camp was much bigger, parents were not invited to performances or events.

Awards

I earned a red tie; that was fun – I was busy.
Betty "Bep" Berger

56

In the early part of the 20th century, camps (mostly boys' camps then) were awash with awards. Most camps had lots of medals, silver cups, and feathers (in keeping with the Indian motif). There were awards for everything – punctuality, neatness, table manners, posture, camp spirit. Leslie Paris says that awards were considered positive reinforcement for good behavior, such as Best Camper and membership in camp honor societies.[25]

However, in a backlash against militarism after the shocking carnage of the first World War, camp administrators and boards in the late 1920s camp world rejected excessive military regimentation in camping, including marching, extreme time management, and the glut of awards.[26] Although the majority of camps still gave awards for "good behavior and special accomplishments,"[27] by the end of the '20s, camp brochures were assuring parents that there would be no semi-military disciplining, no boring routines. In the mid-1930s there was some degree of freedom of choice and a decreased emphasis on badges and awards.

Camp spirit was linked with working for awards at Hagan, although the types and number of awards were many fewer than in those earlier times of camping. "Is everyone working for the camp awards?" *The Queue* asks. The main kind of award was the color ties, colored triangular neckerchiefs, worn instead of the brown straight uniform tie, both always and only tied in a square knot. Anyone could work for these, going from department to department during the activity periods, checking off the requirements as they did them. The first Cricket (red) tie awards went to Dorothy Anstat and Olive Weaver. "Come on you campers," says *The Queue* in early August, "we want to see more of you working for the awards and wearing red ties." The awards most frequently noted in the Queue were swimming levels, denoted by the color caps, as swim tests were given at the end of every two-week session, and Junior Life Saving. Campers were urged to make their parents proud by earning ties and passing swim tests: "You will make your Folks Happy if you Get Your Awards."

Another kind of award, which didn't have a check-off list, was the Best All-Around Camper, selected by the staff. The qualifications, announced in *The Queue* early that first summer, were many: Cooperativeness, Ability, Morale, Promptness, Health, Attitude, Good Sportsmanship, Aim, and Neatness. Some are self-explanatory, though we don't know what to make of "aim." We assume not archery. Perhaps motivation? *The Queue:* "It would be a fine thing if all of our girls could be working toward winning the all-around camper award, too. Let's put our best foot forward and help make this the camp with a character." Awards were given at the closing campfire of each session and reported the next day in *The Queue* with pride and enthusiasm. At the end of the first summer the Best All-Around Camper was Ben Walker. The tie and honor awards were exciting and happy-making but basically serious. On the lighter side was *The Hagan Score*, "Bests" and "Mosts" voted on by the campers. Here, besides the Funniest, Most Original, and Best Sport, for example, were the Biggest Giggler, the Most Freckles, the Slowest, and the Biggest Talker, among several others. Light-hearted, that is, unless perhaps you had been voted the Biggest Pest.

Inspections, as well, were part of the award-and-rules relationship. Cabins were inspected daily. In the 1937 Daily Schedule, Inspection followed the 1:00 Rest Hour. Inspection was carried out by the unit heads who took points off for "dust bunnies" on the floor, beds not tight and neat, shutters not all aligned. In the first season, we hear only about prizes in *The Queue*, not penalties – those would come later. Intermediate 7 got the highest inspection average for one week, 100 %. Their reward was to be in charge of flag raising and retreat for the week. When Senior 2 had the highest average for the week, they had watermelon. Another week, Senior 4 had homemade apple pie. When Camp Miller invited Hagan seniors to see their play, *In Aunt Mahaly's Cabin*, the highest junior and intermediate cabins in Inspection that week got to go along. Every week the Inspection winners were acknowledged during Announcements at breakfast.

What role does inspection play in camp life? Besides keeping cabins neat and clean, and besides teaching girls the value of keeping one's personal spaces neat and clean, inspection also helped create camp culture, with a goal of helping each other.

Along with rules, awards, and inspections, Hagan started with a concept of camper governance inherited from late 19th and early 20th century camping, when campers often planned the day's activities with the counselors. In 1937 at Hagan, the Camp Council was assembled to help staff plan events and apparently to take messages about behavior from the administration back to campers. We don't know precisely what the Camp Council did. It's fairly clear, though, that the girls were not as integrally involved in planning events as boys had been in the early years of camping. *The Queue* urges girls to "bring any problems or questions" to the Camp Council. "This is your camp – help us to make it the very best." The Camp Council met approximately every week. Cabin representatives also were responsible for the Friday issues of *The Queue* itself. But beyond that, there is never any mention of their having much to do with actual camp organization or discipline.

The Weather and the River

Summer in the Poconos runs the gamut from dry to wet, cool to scorching. At the top right of most days' *Queue* the writer gives the weather forecast: "The sun will peep through the clouds, believe it or not." "There will be rain sooner or later." "Continued cool. Ha! Ha!" This last was in a time of a ferocious heat wave and in the same vein, "Continued fair weather but we're hoping for relief soon," and "The sun will be in its usual place."

When it was sunny, everyone was outdoors most of the time. In light rains, as many activities as possible went right on or moved inside briefly. *The Queue* reports that on "the first real rainy day," which was the Friday at the end of the second week, there were 94 girls in Great Hall making things, playing games, doing arts and crafts. "Oh Heck" was a favorite card game (it was, after all, a church camp). The sixth week of camp that first year was rainy all week long. According to *The Queue*,

"The first rainy week was passed quite successfully with everyone keeping those real Camp Hagan smiles on top. Who is afraid of a rainy day?"

"Brrrr!" exclaims *The Queue,* "The water really wasn't as bad as it seemed." After a cool spell in the weather, the water probably was just as bad as it seemed. But Hagan girls were tough, or became tough enough to deal with it, and were sure that growing up with the river increased courage and strength to cope with difficulties.

Hagan campers led a simple, fairly rustic life, and although improvements were made over the years, Hagan life never veered very far from that early environment. As for electricity in the cabins, no, that never appeared, nor did the white monograms on the uniform top. But so much had been accomplished in a few short years! So many campers and counselors lived in the cabins, used the crafts and sports and entertainment facilities, learned reverence for the out-of-doors and gained strength in that learning, and grew spiritually and socially that we must ask: so what's a white monogram or a little electricity in the face of such riches? As director Tay said at the end of the 1939 summer, there were "thankful hearts for all the joys these days have brought."

(Oh, and remember, don't lean on the screen door in Great Hall!)

Endnotes

---

[24] These stories were from the late 19th century, with sentimental but heartwarming themes.

[25] p. 145

[26] Van Slyck, p. 20

[27] Paris, p. 234

Part II: The Middle

1940s and '50

Chapter 6

And Let the Rest of the World Go By

With a camp just like this, it's all peace and bliss
We leave all other things behind and come and find
A camp that's known to God alone, just a camp to call our own...
We'll build a friendship that's true out here 'neath the blue
And let the rest of the world go by.
1948, 1950s, and 1964 Hagan Songbooks

The song "Let the Rest of the World Go By" comes from 1919, after the "Great War." In World War I, more than 38 million were killed or injured, in horrible ways, for reasons unknown to most, and many populations around the world vowed, *Never again.* "And let the rest of the world go by" reflected that view, and this camp version of the song, possibly written for a song contest in the early years of Camp Hagan, shows the long-lasting, if wistful, power of that wish. Many campers speak of Hagan as a place to be away from the world's fears, to work on their own business of growing up and making friends. Parents saw it as a place to keep their children safe, to protect them from growing tensions and then war in Europe, again.

The Second World War, however, would not let the world go by so easily. The Lutheran *Minutes* report that conferences took place with government officials in which "summer camps were asked to continue" their assistance and, "barring an unforeseen military development, would be given necessary supplies and allowances." The U.S. Government asked camps to stay open for the 1944 season, though personnel problems were much worse, along with the same problems of food and supplies under rationing.

By May of 1944, the Camp Committee's report to the Synod made it clear this was "wartime camping," with a ban on pleasure driving, food shortages, and a "pinch on personnel." Despite difficulties, 943 campers from ten states came to Hagan and Miller, and applications for 1945 totaled 1500 for the two camps, much higher than the usual 1100 or so. The Committee reported a "splendid staff" for 1945.

Though the Lutheran Synod asked for patience and cooperation "through these trying times," World War II was not a major focus of activity and attention in the camp summers. The director and the nurse in their white uniforms still greeted campers and parents and gave out cabin assignments. There were still campfires, special days, singing, cabin projects for Evening Program, and tearful departures. After online discussions among elder camper/counselors in 2010, Christine Hill Killough says:

> None of us, Sis [Director Esther Wenrich] included, could remember camp being any different during the war years. . . Just a calm and peaceful place to be away from the worries of war.

When V-J Day arrived in mid-August 1945, it was celebrated joyfully. Posie Bosek Clymer reports, "We paraded all over the campus for hours banging on pots and pans from the kitchen after we got the news."

Otherwise, no one recalls anything ever being mentioned about world or national events. For example, neither the Korean War (1950 – 1953), the Cold War (1946 - 1989), nor social issues such as conformity or prejudice were items for discussion. One reason may be that in those periods, late '40s, '50s at least, and maybe early '60s, parents didn't really want their children burdened or frightened by worldly events. Many campers' families were perhaps not given to these sorts of discussions anyway, at least not with their children. (Progressive camps and families generally paid more attention to social issues.) Dutch (Dorothy Dutcher Logan) says camp was a place to get away from worldly things, a peaceful place in nature.

Surely some campers must have lost uncles, brothers, even fathers, but their grief is not recorded. There must have been private worries, with fathers and brothers in danger and mothers away from home at work. What is preserved is the Lutheran Synod's acknowledgment of and response to the restrictions – financial, material, and personnel – placed on the camps they sponsored. So, except for WWII and hurricanes Connie and Diane in 1955 (more to come on the hurricanes), there was very little knowledge of, or attention to, the happenings of the outside world.

Stability

Camp Hagan had gotten a good start in 1937, '38, and '39. Then what? The 1940s and '50s – the mid-20th century and the middle years of Camp Hagan – were rooted in the first few years, and most of the traditions lasted well into the last decade of Camp Hagan's existence. What made Camp Hagan feel so solid and stable?

We know that the first two directors, Gladys Marie Staub and Jane M. Taylor worked with the staff to provide a smooth-running camp where girls and traditions could be nurtured and grow, with Tay continuing as director until 1945. Although the next director, Betty (Liz Gross), from Teaneck, NJ, was not on the staff previously, sisters Dotty (Dorothy) and Midge (Marjorie) were staff members in the early '40s and when their sister was director. Sis Wenrich made a special mark on these years, with Kit (Kathryn Berger) as associate director for most of that time. Earlier, Sis had been head of athletics, head of the junior unit, and associate director, and Kit had been head of Arts and Crafts and then senior unit. Beloved nurse Skipper (Caroline Boyer) cared for campers' medical needs from 1944-1951(with a couple of years absence). Edy (Edith M. Klain) was Associate Director with Sis after Kit retired and then directed Camp Hagan with Jane Endres, a long-time camper, counselor, and waterfront head, as Associate Director. When Jane Endres was director, Fran (Frances Bowden), an assistant professor of physical education at Wilson College, served as Associate Director. Then, in the last two years of the '50s, Fran Bowden was Hagan's director.

In this genealogy, we can see a source of the remarkable stability in Camp Hagan's program and direction. From the second year on, all of the directors served for two years or more, perhaps not remarkable in itself, but, more importantly, for most it was the culmination of previous years of experience at Hagan, often as campers and then staff. In most cases the associate directors also were experienced campers and counselors at Hagan. The Lutheran Synod saw this as a selling point, noting in the 1949 *Minutes* that most of the staff at both Hagan and Miller would be returning the next season. Campers from the '40s and '50s speak of their feelings of safety in the sameness, stability, and predictability of camp personnel, organization, and practices.

Who were the campers?

From 1940 on, Hagan was home each summer to never fewer than 350 campers, approximately 370 through most of the war, and rising to 408 in 1946, the first year after World War II (see Table 1). After that, the camp population grew steadily to its peak of 661 in 1960. Campers came from several states, at times twelve or fourteen, mainly nearby, especially New York and New Jersey and also Michigan, Ohio, and Georgia, but largely, of course, Eastern Pennsylvania. The Philadelphia area generally sent the most campers, following the well-established principle of summer camps to get children out of the city and into the country. In the war years the number of states represented decreased to eight in 1943, but returned to ten states in 1944, even before the war was over. After that the Synod stopped counting states.

When asked where campers grew up (App. 5), they reported among many others, Camp Hill, Drexel Hill, Hokendauqua, Mechanicsburg, Reading, and Souderton in Pennsylvania, and Woodhaven (Queens), New York City. But a few campers added, "Where did I grow up? At Camp Hagan, of course!"

The Synod's early goal, stated in the 1940 *Minutes,* was "to step in to the lives of young people with a vital, virile Christian message and claim them for the Master," a project aimed more toward the boys' camp than to the girls'. After the first few years of noting "encouraging" increases in Lutheran campers, in 1946 (for the summer of 1945) and after the war

65

was over, the Synod began to note exact numbers at both camps. In the late 1940s the percentage of the Lutheran population at Camp Hagan relative to all campers hovered in the low seventies. After a radical dip to 50% in 1950, the proportion of Lutheran campers was about 65% from 1952 to 1960. [See Table 1]

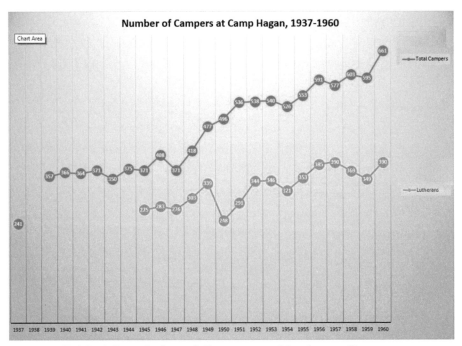

Table 1 Population of Campers and Lutheran Campers

How old were these campers? According to the annual promotional brochures, girls from eight to sixteen could enroll. But we have personal testimony of some campers being brought to camp at seven years, six, even one at five. Campers were divided into Junior, Intermediate, and Senior units. Many young campers (and some older ones) suffered from homesickness. Age affected the camp experience in other ways. For example, Pat Ulrich Ritter returned to camp expecting to be in Intermediate 9 or 10, the oldest intermediate cabins, but, on finding herself assigned to Senior 1, promptly sent home with her parents the three teddy bears she'd brought. On the other hand, girls in the oldest couple of senior cabins, who either didn't apply or were not selected for the Counselor-in-Training program, often would rather sit in the cabins (forbidden), smoke (forbidden), practice make-up techniques, and read magazines.

Why did girls go to camp, and why Camp Hagan?

By the 1940s, many parents had come to believe that attending summer camp was a good thing. In addition, in the late '40s and early '50s, polio outbreaks nationwide led many parents to feel that their children would be safer away from contagion in the cities.[28] Pools and beaches were closed, and the river and mountains might offer less exposure to the illness. The Lutheran Synod says in the 1944 promotional brochure that parents believed that "their daughters needed Camp Hagan especially in wartime."

Various networks provided information about camps among people who knew each other in neighborhoods, in churches, and, of course, families. In contrast, private camps in the post-war years advertised widely. Camping associations, such as the Camp Directors Association or the later American Camp Association, provided information about camps in an industry journal called *Camp Life*, in Porter Sargent's influential yearly *Handbook of Summer Camps,* and in *Redbook* magazine, which had a department just for camping. Soon agency- and organization-sponsored camps, such as the YMCA (Ch. 1), joined in advertising their campsites and programs.

Churches, however, did not enter into commercial publicity. Lutheran churches received notice about Hagan and Miller from the Synod, and word was spread through promotional brochures and through ministers talking to their congregations. Personal reasons for sending children to camp included parents working, illness of parents, or a temporary solution for divorcing families. Whatever their reasons, girls arrived on Saturdays, every two weeks, for two, four, six, and some for the whole eight weeks.

CH sales brochures

How did campers get there?

Girls usually came to Camp Hagan by car but occasionally were picked up in the camp truck from the East Stroudsburg bus or train stations.

World War II rationing impinged on driving. Rationing began in 1942, first with sugar and coffee, and then tires and gas. Gasoline rationing, which later became nationwide, started on the East Coast in May of 1942, thus affecting the 1942 camp season.

Posie Bosek Clymer recalls,

> In order to get to camp during the WWII years, my friend's Dad had a truck for his business and used it to drive us up and back [from the Philadelphia area]. No one else had enough gas.

Jan Mueller says, since there were several girls from the town of Woodhaven, New York, parents put their "A" gas coupons (the most restrictive) together for the trips to and from camp. Dutch Logan remembers the return trip, when she had a bad case of poison ivy:

> When camp closed I had to bounce along in the camp truck, be joined by my brother at Miller, and get a rickety old, hot train [the Delaware/Lackawanna] from the Water Gap to Hoboken, New Jersey where our parents met us. If they had driven all the way to camp they would have used up too many gas ration stamps.

Girls didn't arrive at camp empty-handed. After they were given their cabin assignments, the first task was to get the luggage from the parking lot to the cabins. Parents were not permitted to drive to the cabins. In the early years, heavy wooden wheelbarrows with metal wheels were the only option, which usually required the help of parents or other campers. If there wasn't a wheelbarrow available, then you really needed some helpful muscle to wrestle the bags and trunks to the cabins.

Soon wheelbarrows gave way to dollies, platforms with wheels, pulled by a truck. Girls brought suitcases, trunks, or both, and sometimes carried a pile of blankets and sheets and a pillow, too. Once delivered at the cabin and emptied, luggage was stored in the loft at the back of the cabin.

How did campers live there?

Group living was a new challenge and joy to most campers. The brown, white-trimmed cabins generally housed eleven girls, plus the counselor, and in 1956 the last cabin, Senior 8, was added.[29]

The counselor slept in the first bed on the left, going in. The counselor's corner contained her foot locker, an orange crate with a skirt, called a "jerry," and a candle, usually stuck in a Chianti bottle (with wax of previous candles dripped down the sides of the basket). Girls eyed these wonders longingly, hoping to some day be a counselor with a spread like that. Other beds were arranged in pairs, heads at opposite ends. Bunk beds were installed at the back on both sides. Some girls preferred those top bunks because they could keep their trunk nearby in the loft and have access to more than the cubbies would hold (and secret snacks), not subject to inspection.

Each girl had a few small wooden shelves nailed between structural two-by-fours in the wall at her bed for personal items. The inside had no other wall finishing. Towels were kept on the iron railing at the end of the bed toward the aisle, always with "folds to the door," so that loose edges were never visible from the front or in danger of blowing off in the unlikely event of a big wind.

In the back of the cabin, behind walls separating the sleeping area, was a walk-in closet on the left – one or two nails for each camper to hang jackets, rainwear, and a dress for the seniors for the Camp Miller dance, with boots and shoes underneath on the floor. In the center back, each girl got one or two box-like shelves, called "cubbies," for clothing and towels. Again, "folds to the door" prevailed. Finally, in the back of the cabin on the right were the little sink, with a wooden shelf above, and the toilet, known as "the john." As there was no electricity in the cabins, campers got ready for bed by flashlight.

The sides of the cabins were open half way up, with wooden shutters pulled up by ropes fastened around a cleat. They were kept at full and even height, day and night, except in rain. Many campers remember the sound of the rain on the roof and on the partially closed shutters. If they were part way open, they still must be kept even. Once, after a Play Day at nearby Camp Akiba, Haganites rode home in the camp truck, awestruck: They had *screens*!

After unpacking and putting clothes, all with hand sewn name labels, into cubbies, campers had to learn how to make a Hagan bed. Sheets (twin-size) were laid as on ordinary beds, pulled tight and smooth, and the bottoms made with square corners, as used in the military (also called hospital corners). This was not easy to do on sagging mattresses, which were replaced gradually, occasionally, over the years. Springs were there forever. "Sagging" is generous for the springs, which had pretty much sprung.

After the sheets, a light blanket could be placed the same way if desired. The interesting, and possibly unique, part of the Hagan bed was the arrangement of the top two blankets. The benefit of using two blankets was that you could pull up just the flap, the folded-down part of the bottom blanket, without messing up the entire bed for rest hour on a chilly day. Also,

Jan Mueller with
Hagan blanket
2016

70

the camp news sheet, *The Queue* or later the *Hagan Herald,*[30] could be kept there for easy reference. Mail and magazines could be stored, if they were flat, under the bottom blanket. (And comic books.)

The nearly obsessive, almost military neatness of Hagan bedmaking and "folds to the door" comforted some campers, perhaps providing an alternative to the chaos of their own home or school or general growing up. For others, however, it was an affront. The '50s, after all, was an odd mix of individualism, fear of mob action, and conformity. Enforced conformity conflicted with individualism, but individualism never outranked conformity. For girls who were conscious of working their way through this conundrum, the emphasis on bedmaking and towel folding seemed at best petty, at worst, rigidly authoritarian. On the other hand, most staff and campers, if they thought about it, believed a tidy environment to be integral to the success of eleven or more girls and a counselor living closely in a small space. And indeed, many campers enjoyed the ritualistic nature of Hagan bedmaking, feeling it to be special to camp and possibly to this camp.

We do not know what the source was for "folds to the door" or Hagan-style beds, but military is a likely guess.

Who helped?

It's impossible to exaggerate the importance of staff. The administration relied on counselors to make the camp work, and campers relied on counselors to help them through their time there. They were relational pairs– counselors implied campers, campers implied counselors. You didn't get one without the other, as each needed the other to fulfill their roles. It was really staff who created the camp experience, organizing activities, enforcing rules, and befriending and counseling campers.

In the World War II years, camps found it hard to find and retain staff. Men were enlisted or drafted, and women now could get better-paying jobs. To solve the problem of attracting qualified personnel, the Lutheran Synod started to seek younger or older Lutheran men and women, that is, not of draft age. People in education were especially desirable because they would have the summers free. The Lutheran Synod felt that the camp salaries were comparable to other "summer work," though Robin Fidler Brancato reports having to skip a year as counselor to earn more money for college.

.

1940 Staff

1951 Staff

Counselors had contact with campers in two main ways, as cabin counselor and as a counselor in a particular department, such as Arts and Crafts or Athletics.

Cabin counselors helped campers along the path of their main job, that of growing up, sometimes directly, offering support and advice, more often just by being there, providing models. They helped girls navigate camp schedules and activities, and sometimes mediated friendships. They guided their cabin groups through Morning Watch and Cabin Devotions, and after Taps many came around to each bed, in the dark, to say goodnight and perhaps answer a question or receive a private confidence. One of campers' main worries each summer was whether they would like their counselor. Most did.

In the mid-20th century the Lutheran Synod hired mostly kind, responsible young women, usually of college age, who had a particular skill, such as athletics or dramatics. Some older women, such as Pinky (Ruth Weidenheimer), head of Arts and Crafts and then Senior Unit head, and Kit Berger, head of Arts and Crafts, then Senior Unit, and for several years Associate Director, stayed on at Hagan and are fondly remembered.

Staff Had a Sense of Humor 1954

73

Counselors had responsibilities that campers didn't see. Administration and department heads came for *pre*-Pre-Camp week. Counselors arrived for Pre-Camp week, to do work needed to reclaim the campsite and cabins from the winter. They got to know each other, and talked about the Hagan way of doing things. Mainly they painted boats and canoes, pulled weeds, lined the tennis courts and other courts and fields, and generally got camp ready to open. Department heads had earlier ordered supplies, such as materials for Arts and Crafts. At the end of the season, after campers left, counselors wrapped mattresses in brown paper and men from Miller helped get them into the loft for storage. Still the mice got to them and once, at camp opening, a snake was found curled up on a mattress. After camp, the waterfront had to be brought up – raft, ropes, blocks for weights for the ropes and raft, boats and canoes, and the buddy board, again with Miller's help. The trucked-in sand from the beginning of the summer was left to wash away into the Delaware in winter storms and spring high waters, and more would be brought in next June.

Cabin counselors lived with the girls assigned to their cabins. Some department heads and staff lived in special cabins or quarters dotted around the campus. The Stables, next to the Senior Unit, eventually had a john, but until the mid-'50s, residents famously had to use the two-seater (no stalls) in the shower house behind Senior Unit. As Phyllis Wiest Gilbert put it, "Two thrones with no privacy." The office staff, often not well known to campers, at first consisted of only the Registrar in 1940, then, by 1955, the Registrar, two office clerks, and the Storekeeper, in charge of the Canteen. In the mid-'50s an assistant nurse joined the medical staff.

Counselors frequently had official nicknames. Many years later Hannelore Freyberg Blew heard someone call "Laurie" after church and knew it had to be someone from Hagan, the only place she was ever known that way. Some campers had nicknames, too, though not as many as counselors: Peaches, (source unknown), Genius (wore glasses and was also smart), and Twinnie (when you didn't know which one you were talking to).

Many camps had Counselor-in-Training (CIT) and Junior Counselor (JC) programs. Hagan's began in 1940, considered by the Synod as leadership training. The JC program started with two girls and grew to six as the camp population steadily increased. JCs were unpaid staff, listed in the Memory Books, and included in the staff picture. They worked in their department and filled in for cabin counselors on their days off. The ten or so CITs, along with five JCs and the Head of CITs, lived in four tents, usually four to a tent, in back of the Senior Unit, called Shanty Town. It was lots of fun for fifteen and sixteen-year olds to be CITs, and it was an honor to be chosen. But there was not much real training involved. This was no fault of the Heads of CITs but rather fairly typical of attitudes toward parenting and teaching at the time. CITs were assigned to one or two cabins to help out when needed and had a major department and a minor department where they spent their days.

I was among the first C.I.T.'s – we got to move out of our Senior Bunks and into the 2 tents up on wooden platforms out in back of Senior amp. Had a few special privileges, "days off," later nights.
Norie McIlvaine Clague

During Sis Wenrich's years as director (1948-1952), only girls who had earned the White Tie, the highest senior award, were eligible to be CITs, and they would ordinarily serve two years as CIT and one year as JC before being hired as counselor. Before and after Sis's directorship, however, CITs were sometimes hired directly as counselors, or the oldest campers became CITs or even JCs without having earned the White Tie. Posey Bosek Clymer, for example, who moved after two years as CIT directly to cabin counselor of an intermediate cabin (she was just out of high school), says that some of the campers were taller than she, but she managed pretty well.

CITs advanced knowledge and skills in their major and minor departments. However, in the '40s and '50s, most CITs and many JCs

75

did not feel very well prepared to be counselor to a cabin full of eleven or twelve girls. Ruth Clegg Whitsel describes being a counselor her first year in a very junior cabin as "flying by the seat of my pants and not even seventeen yet."

Counselors and JCs had a well-earned day off each week, CITs less often. For their day off, six or so counselors, JCs, and CITs generally rode into East Stroudsburg on the camp truck early in the morning, napped in the room reserved for them by the camp at the American House – actually a rooming house – shopped at Wycoff's department store, often went to a movie (Yul Brynner in *The King and I* was a favorite), had dinner, perhaps at the Town Tavern, and returned at night in the camp truck. Counselors worked hard, on duty day and night for eight weeks, plus pre- and post-camp detail. One perk to counselor life was the occasional night swims for counselors.

Counselors had authority, offering comfort for skinned knees or hurt feelings as well as providing guidance and discipline. Children whose own home lives did not offer much in the way of emotional comfort benefitted especially from this combination. However, counselors were oftentimes not more than a few years older than the oldest campers and were not done with concerns of their own growing up. In *Children's Nature*, Leslie Paris explains that "counselors represented an intermediate generation, in some ways like parents, in other ways like older peers."[31]

Campers may not have been aware of it, but counselors of any age were sometimes distracted by conditions in their own lives. Thus, events such as Camper/Counselor Day, where campers and counselors switched roles, had special resonance. This festivity appears to have occurred at most all camps at some time or other, with reports that counselors behaved worse than campers ever did, and campers ran wild.[32]

Like the teenagers that many counselors were, some misbehaved without the permission of a special day. For serious misbehavior, counselors could be fired. Sis Wenrich said she only ever had to dismiss one counselor, after warnings, who stayed out too late and came back to camp drunk.

Counselors taught campers skills, for example, how to paddle a canoe, to swim, to use a wood burning tool, to recognize trees and plants (especially poison ivy), and to understand the rules of games and to participate as well as possible. And always, always, the counselors, from JCs to the director, were role models for growing girls. This is how you behave. This is how to share what you know. This is how to grow up.

Alums remember their counselors. Not everybody can be wonderful, but most campers agree that, overall, Camp Hagan staff was really, really good and contributed over many years to campers' wellbeing and development.

"Shanty Town"

The floor is gray, there are cracks and ridges.
The tent side rails are like long gray bridges
Upon which are hung in various array
A flashlight, a clipboard that's seen better days.
A washcloth, a whistle, a bathing cap (green),
And also a Kleenex box there can be seen.
And then there's the bed. If you're lucky it's not
Exactly the hardest of broken-springed cots.
A trunk and a jerry, an orange crate, too,
While under the bed lies many a shoe.
Ah yes! from the middle, attached to four ropes,
Hang all of our clothes bags (and also our hopes!)
This is our tent, the best place in camp,
And who really cares if the laundry gets damp,
Or the fact that the canvas, when wet, usually leaks?
For better or worse, it's our home for eight weeks.

Alice Royer Roy, age 15, 1953

Endnotes

---

[28] CDC http://www.cdc.gov/features/poliofacts/ 7/20/14

[29] We don't know when the additional junior cabins after the original 8 were built.

[30] For a few years in the mid '40s known as the *Walkie Talkie*.

[31] Paris, p. 134

[32] Paris, p. 148, 111

Chapter 7

Summer Days

Morning mist. Getting awake early –
snuggling down under the covers and watching
the mist drift between the cabins.
Jane Detwiler Levan

Perhaps the best way to "see" life at Camp Hagan in the '40s and '50s is to picture the events of a typical day, which involved activity and rest, fun and meditation, group and individual activity, indoors and outdoors. Campers woke to Reveille, played by a bugler, if there was one that year, or over the loudspeaker from a recording. *The Queue* (daily news sheet) reported on August 13, 1941, "Every time we look there is a different person blowing the bugle, but they're doing a swell job." Reveille was at 7:15 from 1940 on. Campers donned uniforms and boots over their shoes for the early morning dew. Many girls were in awe of one counselor who, for several years, wore high fitted boots in the damp morning and evenings. Jackets or sweatshirts were often necessary – for instance, in August of 1941 the nighttime low was about forty degrees.

Campers put on clean uniforms Wednesdays and Sundays, the tops no longer tucked in (Ch. 2). Though the

Intermediates' uniforms on a
Tuesday, 1949

outfits were not very stylish, they were also not very expensive ($2.30

delivered in 1940, up from $2.00 in 1937, and in 1956, $3.50) and they held up well. The uniforms gave parents, the administration, and the Synod the much-desired harmony of appearance, and benefitted campers in that nobody had to think about what to wear or what anyone else would wear.

Why brown and tan? Who knows. The very first uniforms were in fact a much lighter tan than later. Some girls were able to get them as hand-me-downs from friends or relatives who had been at Camp Hagan in the first years, 1937 on, and they were much coveted. In the '50s, some older girls wore their shorts rolled up high and "pegged" with a complicated twist that kept coming un-pegged. Laundry was generally sent home in boxes or laundry mail cases to be brought back when parents visited on change weekends. Some used the Keipers laundry service from East

Rolled-up pants came unrolled

Stroudsburg. A good Pennsylvania Dutch name, it unfortunately rhymed with diapers, giving Camp Miller material for good-natured satiric songs.

> *I was very lucky and had Connie Kline's old, almost white uniforms because our fathers had been friends in the little town of Northampton.*
> Alice

Once dressed, girls went out on the front porch of the cabin for Morning Watch, or Matins as it was called until 1947. In 1942 Matins was moved to 7:40. Each day's entry in the *Morning Watch* mimeographed booklets consisted of a Bible reading and a brief tale with a clear moral, perhaps a little discussion of its meaning, and a prayer. A few campers found Morning Watch time unsatisfying because most of the entries had to serve both younger and older campers. For example, a

81

1953 *Morning Watch* shows that stories sometimes began with "Once upon a time there was a very happy king," or "Reuben lived back in Bible times." Still, most campers found the gentle, meditative ten minutes or so a good beginning to the day.

Flag Raising sounded at 7:50, and campers came to the triangle around the flag pole in front of Great Hall, juniors and intermediates on one side, seniors on the second side, and the director and counselors at the base of the triangle. The flag was carried and raised by the Honor Guard, made up of Honor Council members. After the Pledge of Allegiance, campers went into Great Hall for breakfast at 8:00. The morning schedule remained this way, with minor five-minute adjustments, for many years.

Mealtime in Great Hall

The tables in Great Hall were square, big old heavy things, seating eight, a counselor and seven campers. There was a bit of a rush on entering because campers wanted to sit with their favorite counselors, Juniors in front of the big fireplace, Intermediates in the middle, and

Seniors at the far end. Campers remained standing at their places to sing grace. A much-loved grace was "God has created a new day, silver and green and gold. Live that the sunset may find us worthy His gifts to hold."

Girls were seated, with much noise from dragging a couple of hundred metal folding chairs. Each senior cabin sent two girls for waitressing Kaper, who carried trays with family-style serving dishes from the kitchen serving-window and cleared up afterward. Breakfasts consisted of hot cereal, scrambled eggs, pancakes, or dry cereals in little individual boxes that frequently leaked. Slim's French toast was very popular, and Joe's cinnamon buns on Sundays were considered the best ever. Beverages were milk or cocoa poured from silvery aluminum pitchers. While the tables were being cleared, campers sang songs and then heard the day's announcements from the director or associate. Announcements occasionally included a thank you to campers' parents who had sent forbidden food items, a box of chocolates for instance, which the staff had unapologetically enjoyed. From 1940 to 1947, breakfast took only half an hour. This seems rather rushed, and from 1948 on, breakfast was allotted an hour.

Cabins were cleaned every morning after breakfast, with chores known as "Kapers." The word probably comes from the military KP: Kitchen Patrol or Kitchen Police, as in "policing the area." The Kaper Chart, prepared by the cabin counselor and posted on the back of the door of each cabin, listed all the tasks, such as sweeping the floor, cleaning the john, taking out the trash, tightening and neatening the ropes in back of the cabins where swim suits were hung, and

Shutters Up and Even 1948

making sure shutters were even, beds tight and corners squared, and all towels and clothes showed folds to the door.

The Kaper Chart was constructed so that each camper in the cabin rotated through all the jobs. Waitress duty – go in early, set up the dishes, bowls, and tableware, carry heavy trays from kitchen window to table, and then take all the dishes back to the kitchen window and clean up the tables, all three meals – was nobody's favorite Kaper. Although counselors usually wouldn't permit switches, some campers tried, especially a senior camper who tried everything she could to trade with someone when she had waitress duty because one of the kitchen staff was interested in her and she didn't know how to deal with that. (Campers were not to fraternize with the "kitchen boys.")

One of the Kapers was "O.D." – Officer of the Day – whose job it was to make sure that everything got done well. Once campers were out at the morning's activities, the unit head inspected the cabins each day, usually rigorously.

Inspection in the '40s and '50s had a new twist. Where originally there were rewards for cabins with good scores, now if results were unsatisfactory, cabinmates must also share in the penalty. At the end of the week the lowest scoring cabins were required to do tasks such as peeling potatoes during World War II and later scrubbing the floor or porches in Great Hall. One camper, Ann Lentz Partlow, laments that her intermediate cabin was last in inspection every week. The Great Hall floors job entailed moving the chairs and tables and mopping, a big job in a room that seated more than 200 people.

In 1940 and '41, a half hour was allotted to Kapers, not much time. Campers in later years may be surprised to learn that from 1942 to 1945 the schedule allowed for an hour and a quarter, then an hour, then 45 minutes, as it remained from1948 to 1969. Although some campers fretted under the expectation of neatness and cleaning, Dutch Logan writes that things were much stricter at home and she was fine with it.

Campers from the late '40s and early '50s remember Kit ringing the bell on the Rat Trap porch for instructional periods and for all activities that weren't signaled by bugle calls. The campers visited Aquatics, Arts and Crafts, Athletics, Entertainment, Nature, Pioneering, and Religion.

Instructional Periods

The basic unyielding camp rule was *Nobody in the cabins in the daytime*. Except, of course, Rest Hour, Free Period, and twice a day changing into or out of swim suits. So, when the bell was rung for start of the first period in the morning, *everybody* left the cabins. The instructional periods were about 45 minutes long, and aside from swimming, which was scheduled by ability levels in the morning and by units in the afternoon, campers could, until the late '50s, choose to do whatever they wanted. Many worked on tie requirements in these times.

The **Aquatics** department originally included boating and canoeing as well as swimming, but these later were separated. Instructional swimming periods in the morning were still referred to by the cap colors indicating Red Cross swimming ability levels. Although white caps earlier had signaled advanced and life-saving class swimmers, in the early '40s this changed so that white caps were worn by those girls who could not swim at all or were "white advanced," able to doggy paddle. Red caps were beginners, yellow caps – intermediates, and blue and green caps – advanced swimmers and Red Cross Life Savers. Until 1955, the motto of the Hagan Aquatics program was "Every Girl a Swimmer." From 1956 on, the goal as expressed in the promotional brochure was slightly less ambitious: for every girl to become safe and comfortable in the water. In the '50s, the White Star category was added for girls who were afraid of the water. A CIT or JC worked with White Stars one-on-one to help them overcome their fear. One girl hated swimming because she was afraid but credits her teacher with reducing her fears and encouraging her so that she passed the Beginner's test and later became a Waterfront counselor. Grace Trimmer LeFevre recalls, "I was always afraid of water, but Dottie [Gross?] convinced me, with her beside me, to swim to the raft."

Swim Buddies

Sometimes, by special arrangement, a group of campers had a skinny dip.

Safety was vigorously maintained, with waterfront counselors in row boats along the ropes that marked the swim areas, and by the buddy board system (Ch. 4). Swim buddies held up their hands when the whistle blew.

Waterfront staff had to contend with the level of the river in severe rains. Water pageants, water carnivals, canoe trips, as well as regular swim classes, had to be postponed or canceled if the river was on a rampage. If the weather was extremely hot, there might be an extra swim added; if it was very cold, swimming instruction might be canceled. Although in the first year the Promotional Brochures claimed that "Camp Hagan has one of the finest beaches along the Delaware River," Hagan alums might not agree. In 1940 the promotional brochure settled for "one of the finest waterfront programs in the Poconos," and with that most former campers and certainly waterfront counselors would agree. But the riverbed was rocky. That was a permanent fixture, though swimmers brought out little stones and tossed them on a pile in a continued attempt at waterfront improvement.

The Aquatics department provided various water events such as carnivals and pageants. Water ballet in the Delaware might seem impossible, but one year, in the mid-'50s, swimmers put on a synchronized swim show, river current and all. The river had a lot to do with making Hagan campers the adults they became.

Boating and canoeing

Red caps, having passed their beginners' test, found that rowing backwards and turning the boat seemed complicated at first, and then it was easy. Canoeing, more demanding, required intermediate-level swimmers. Campers learned the vocabulary – thwarts and gunnels (older: gunwales, pronounced the same) and the specialized roles of bow and stern paddles, along with the proper strokes for each. The test for canoeing certification included capsizing the canoe, learning that you could breathe in the space under the canoe, and righting it again. The awards were little felt cut-out canoe shapes and boat shapes.

The canoes were wooden frames covered with canvas, painted brown, with the camp logo in white on the bow. They were very heavy, and waterfront counselors recall lugging them up onto the beach and chaining them at the end of the day. Bringing them the forty feet up the boat slide to campus at the end of the season was much harder and required Miller muscle to accomplish.

Some campers were canoe nuts who went on every trip and tried to get more scheduled. Canoe trips seem to have been either wonderful or awful, as the special pages "Memories of Canoe Trips" show. However, even the occasional semi-disastrous trip didn't discourage most enthusiasts.

Ruth Clegg Whitsel and I were almost always canoeing partners. I was useless at trying to right a capsized canoe. She pretty much did it for us.
Alice

87

> *I didn't know anything about mural art and I always worried about that girl diving into the steps in the 1948 Aquatics mural.*
> Alice

Arts and Crafts

This department gave campers a wide array of things to make and crafts to learn. Lanyards were very popular, made of gimp (flat plastic cord in many colors). Emma Hallman Mele, an artist in her own right, says:

> *Lanyards, lanyards, and more lanyards.*
> *I've taught every one of my five kids how to make them (and grandkids).*

There were wooden boxes of all sizes to carve or paint, ceramics, including a kiln, which produced pins and other small objects, felt – to create bags and stuffed animals, canvases for oil painting, leather links, to make a belt, and tiny purses of leather to sew up with gimp. There was a good jigsaw to make shapes, or pins, out of wood. A new Arts and Crafts building was built in 1957, according to the 1958 Lutheran *Minutes.*[33]

Arts and Crafts Shop, 1948

> *I never could remember how to make the sliding box on a lanyard – my friend Ruth always did it for me.*
> Alice

The much-loved murals, eight feet by four feet, created each year in the Craft building and mounted above the windows in Great Hall, surrounded campers at mealtimes. Each mural was a collaborative project, with the head of Arts and Crafts, the director, and associate director (especially if she was an artist herself, like Kit Berger) choosing a subject, the head and counselors of Arts and Crafts drafting the design, and all the A and C staff along with interested campers and counselors helping with the painting. The mural subjects reflected departmental activities, special days, or the camp goals, to Socially Broaden, Physically Fortify, and Spiritually Deepen. The subjects were kept secret until unveiling, but campers could go and see if they put in some time painting.

Athletics

Camp Hagan managed to make a wide range of athletics enjoyable for almost all campers, regardless of natural abilities. In the early '40s horseback riding was a very popular activity. Advanced riders first thing in the morning were taken in the Hagan-Miller truck to the barn down the road, which later became the family/religious instruction camp, Ministerium, and then rode the horses back to Hagan for various levels of riding instruction. The apex of the horse riding each year was a walk, trot, and canter show. There was no jumping. To the sorrow of many campers, riding was discontinued after World War II.

Athletic equipment was initially stored in the Rat Trap, with baseball bats behind the door. In the early '50s, the Chicken Coop, a little shed (that had indeed been a chicken coop) between the entrance road and Great Hall, housed the bats, hockey sticks, box hockey equipment, and balls for all the various games. Near the Chicken Coop were also the tetherball pole, box hockey, and a much-used drinking fountain. Campers got used to the minerally mountain water.

> *When I was about 12, a girlfriend and I cleaned out a chicken coop for a playhouse. It was a terrible job, and we never played there. All respect to whoever cleaned out that chicken coop for Camp Hagan.*
> Alice

Physical education became an important part of American culture, especially through the teachings of John Dewey, and by the 1930s most states had compulsory physical education requirements. By the '40s and '50s, this had been more or less codified into physical education classes a couple of times a week and trying out for whatever sports teams your school had, if you were good enough. How were Hagan athletics different?

Earlier we noted that the Aquatics motto was "Every Girl a Swimmer," but in the Athletics Department the goal could not be for every girl to be an athlete. Not everybody could hit a bullseye in archery (or even the target!), or catch a fly ball, make a field hockey goal, or slam a ping pong ball. At Hagan, the emphasis was on trying, improving, building skills and confidence from wherever you began. A camper never had to stand around waiting to be the last one picked, an experience which many recalled all too well from schoolyard games and physical education classes. Campers learned that when you try something, you may in fact not learn completely how to do it but you'll be better at it, wherever you started from. At Hagan you learned that you could try and, most important, be safe trying.

Some girls who arrived already skilled at one sport or another, such as softball, were able to advance their skills and learn other games as well.

Pioneering and Nature

The camping movement in America was rooted in a desire to connect with nature, and thus Camp Hagan emphasized Pioneering and Nature in the Hagan experience. In Pioneering, originally called Campcraft or Woodscraft, campers learned how to tie knots, make a campfire, use an ax, and make bedrolls. Making a bedroll and keeping it rolled were important arts in overnight hiking. Modern instructions include a foam mattress, a sleeping bag, and a pillow, but such luxuries were not part of the experience in the '40s and '50s. After all, pioneers had only blankets.

The head of Pioneering organized hikes to Sunrise Lake near Dingman's Ferry, brother and sister hikes with Camp Miller, and all overnight hikes and canoe trips. A frequent overnight hike went to the Ministerium Camp. It was not a glamorous campsite, but campers remember the fun of cooking breakfast outdoors before hiking back to Hagan.

I hated hikes, especially overnight hikes!
Patty Pirrault Anderson

Probably the most difficult hike Hagan campers took was the trek to Hidden Lake, now called Sunfish Pond, a glacial lake on the Appalachian Trail in a hardwood forest along the Kittatinny Ridge. Miller always canoed Hagan campers across the Delaware from their camp to the Jersey side and ferried them back at the end of the day. In contrast, the little trek into Bushkill with a bag supper of meat and cheese sandwiches and an apple or a plum was a hike all cabins took about every two weeks. Winona (Five) Falls was also a popular hike. And although Patty Pirrault hated hikes, she returned to Hagan for many summers.

In the Nature Department campers maintained the nature walk along the river bank and learned to identify plants, birds, and constellations, and made spatter prints, where you laid a leaf or fern on a piece of paper, then scrubbed tempura paint through the screen with a tooth brush to make the outline. The results were lovely and very individual.

Religion

Activities of the Religion Department figured importantly in every camper's day. The Religion Department supplied the *Morning Watch* booklets. Campers helped with Vespers and Church schedules and took part in Vespers services. For many years Sunday evening entertainment was "Campers' Own," a skit night based on Biblical stories. As a Lutheran camp, Hagan of course included a spiritual dimension, especially services and devotions, but less Bible study and evangelism than that of later church camps.

In 1950, the Religion requirements for the White Tie were to take part in two Vesper Services, help plan and participate in a Camper's Own, lead a Cabin Devotion, and make a personal devotional booklet. The Religion counselor oversaw all of these and helped campers to fulfill their requirements, which shifted slightly over the years, more radically in the late '50s. In the last years of the '50s, religion classes appeared in each cabin's daily schedule, unknown in the '40s and most of the '50s.

> *[In my first year, as a junior,] the counselor at my breakfast table made me eat oatmeal.   I threw up (perhaps out of spite?)   and to this day cannot or will not touch the awful stuff!*
> Ginny Hausmann Fitzgerald

Dinner

After three instructional periods in the morning, forty-five minutes were allotted to dinner in 1954. This meal was actually an old-fashioned main meal at noon consisting of meat (extremely well done and sliced very thin), potatoes, especially mashed, with canned vegetables (some campers recall stewed tomatoes), and maybe salad (though no one can actually remember any). Not fancy, but plentiful. The counselor at a table dished out food on light green or tan Boonton Company (then located in New Jersey) Melmac (melamine) dishes. There was bread at every meal, which had to be broken into four pieces. Every camper had to eat at least a bite of everything. Picky eaters at home often found that they ate most everything at camp without much fuss. (There was no payoff for fuss at camp.) Meals were fun, filled with laughter and singing. Thursdays was usually the occasion for chicken chow mein, canned, topped with canned dried noodles, which was not universally loved. Phyl Wiest Gilbert disliked it so much that she made sure she sat at a table where she knew the counselor wouldn't insist on her eating it.

Peanut butter was a staple, and apple butter was much liked. Fish on Friday, maybe not so much.

"Bug juice," described in *The Marine Corps Dictionary* online as "colored, sweetened water," was super-sweet, made from artificially flavored powder, and appeared without fail at dinner and supper. The on-line *Urban Dictionary* points out that it was "commonly served on US Navy vessels in the enlisted men's mess and can also be used to clean brass." Hagan Campers (and children at many other camps) happily drank this concoction. Bug juice was Kool-Aid. The early Kool-Aid boxes had a picture of Bugs Bunny on them. And that's how it got the name of bug juice.

Songs and Singing

And those stupid songs!
a one-year, non-Hagan camper

Maybe not stupid, but certainly often very silly. "We're here because we're here" came close to fitting the non-camper's evaluation above. Note that when Camp Hagan began in 1937, Tin Pan Alley, which gave us such gems as *moon, croon, June* and *spoon*, was coming to a close. And songs such as "I'm a Lonely Little Petunia in an Onion Patch" from the 1940s and the *Witch Doctor* in the '50s who said "Ooh ee ooh ah ah, ting tang walla walla ting tang" showed that pop songs in this period could be pretty silly, too.

Most singing was done during dessert or after, but campers recall singing at the beginning "Here we sit like birds in the wilderness, waiting for the food to come." Also, there was a teasing reminder about manners in "Nancy, Nancy, strong and able, get your elbows off the table," spoken (or yelled) in unison. Campers agree, it was in fun, not hurtful. Other old favorites: "The More We Get Together, "Slap! Bang!, Here Again," and "You Can't Ride in My Little Red Wagon." The circular "Rain would be such dreary weather, had we nothing else but Rain would be..." was oddly satisfying during the rainy periods that usually occurred at least once every summer.

"John Jacob Jingleheimer Schmidt" was still around, and for a few years in the '50s some manic singing of the Mickey Mouse Club theme song prevailed. "My Hat, It Has Three Corners" was a motion song in which gradually key words were replaced by appropriate gestures. Other motion songs such as "Peter Paul Hagan Wears a Flower in His Lapel" worked similarly. (At the Lutheran Theological Seminary in Philadelphia there is in fact a picture of Peter Paul Hagan, donor of the land for Camp Hagan, with a flower in his lapel. Phyllis Wiest Gilbert and Pat Ulrich Ritter found this picture when they were permitted to make copies of the Lutheran *Minutes* for this book.)

Many songs came from wars or military groups, some very old, adapted for singing at camp. "Dewey was an Admiral" came from the Spanish-American War, 1898, and "Mary Margaret Truman" signaled the period after 1945. By the time of the late '40s and '50s, songs from World War II had made their way into the repertory, for example, "Gee Mom, I Wanna Go Home," substituting "Camp Hagan" for "the Army." "Chester, Have You Heard about Harry? He just got back from the Army" was another motion song. Campers in these years also enjoyed some old folk songs – "Clementine," "Cockles and Mussels," as well as spirituals such as "Sit Down, Sister," "Dem Bones," and "Noah, He Built an Ark." We might guess that singing together was such fun, it didn't matter much what the words were. Campers and counselors alike sang "Oh it was sad, oh it was sad, it was sad when the great ship went down," with absolutely no notion of the disaster (the *Titanic*) it represented.

Ruth Clegg Whitsel recalls being told to be sensitive to the juniors with the singing. The youngsters sang slowly, and everyone else sang too fast for them, for example, "I'm a Little Teapot" with motions. Occasionally two songs were going at once.

Lovely serious songs were reserved for campfire.

Rest Hour

Dinner, singing, then Rest Hour, usually an hour, though in the last few years of the '50s, it was listed inexplicably in the schedule for an hour and a half. At first, campers had to lie flat on their beds for the whole time. Later, seniors could read quietly in the second half, no talking. Counselors, unfortunately, didn't dare sleep, lest pandemonium erupt. Pat Ulrich Ritter, in response to a question about Rest Hour, said "Can't remember!!!" But other cabinmates remember the time at Rest Hour when Pat reached down to get something on the floor, leaning on both arms with her body half off the bed, and the counselor, Janie Endres, grinning good-naturedly (and perhaps a tad wickedly) made her stay that way to the end of Rest Hour.

During or at the end of Rest Hour, mail was delivered, including "Miller mail," which might be between brothers and sisters, but might also arise from romantic contacts made at Hagan-Miller dances.

Afternoon

For many years there were three instructional periods in the afternoon as well as in the morning. However, in 1957, to accommodate the extended Rest Hour, only two activity periods fit in the schedule. Campers went to free swim with their unit – Juniors, Intermediates, and

Seniors. In the mid-'50s the whole program changed, with campers moving through the morning and afternoon periods in their cabin groups. We can see that this arrangement would be good for cabin spirit and cohesion, as well as for scheduling of activities for department heads, but some campers missed the process of figuring out on their own their tie requirements and setting up a plan to get them done and signed by the department heads.

Free Period

After all that structured activity, Free Period was a welcome respite, at first for an hour then from 1948 on a little less. What went on in Free Period? Chatting, writing letters, singing, and in the late '40s and early '50s strumming ukuleles. Twice a week at Free Period campers could go to the Rat Trap to buy their canteen books. For many years, the *Memory Books* show Free Period as also the time for Counselor Swim, though no one recalls doing that. Some

Below: Pat Ulrich,
Ruth Clegg, Alice Royer,
Bobbie Miller, Rosie Hallman,
Judy Jester

Pyramids were popular
JCs 1948 from top, left to right: Allie (Alice) Beck (Head),
Laurie (Hanelore) Freydburg,
Patty Pirall,
Carol Mason, Chris Hill,
Mollie (Eleanor) Miller

96

counselors preferred gathering in the Stables and smoking. Campers didn't officially know what counselors weren't officially doing, of course, but the wisps of smoke coming out around closed shutters gave them away.

There was some occasion for a little conflict here, because if campers really liked their cabin counselor, they wanted her with them for Free Period. In their view, Free Period was for campers, not counselors.

Free Period could also be a time for reading. The camp had a library, added in 1953 on some shelves in the Korn Kribbe and staffed by senior camper volunteers. The library didn't get much use – Hagan was such an active place, the environment didn't really support lying around reading.

Call to Retreat

Campers were called by bugle or recording to Flag Lowering. The Honor Guard folded the flag into the military triangle. It was a solemn moment, except when occasionally someone fainted. Dehydrated, probably, even though on very hot days salt pills were handed out.

Supper and Canteen

Campers don't remember much difference between dinner and supper

Girls just wanna have fun
From bottom: Ruth Clegg, Carol Ann McDaniels, Nora
Erhrig, Alice Royer, Sue McDaniels

except perhaps cold cuts, which usually translated to bologna. A favorite grace before supper was "Evening is here, the board is spread. Thanks be to God who gives us bread." Until 1945 only thirty-five minutes was scheduled for supper, in 1945, fifty minutes, and finally in 1950, one hour. As at dinner, campers ate and sang. Menu items seemed about the same, and so did the songs. There was a lot of singing. After supper there tended to be a stampede to get out to the canteen line, and occasionally in the *Hagan Herald* a reprimand appeared.

Tournaments

Two, four, six, eight,
Who do we appreciate?
Cabin 4, Cabin 4, Yaaaay!

Following Canteen, the whole camp played in or went to Tournaments. While most activities challenged campers to improve personal skills or learning, tournaments fostered team sports and sportsmanship. These were competitive sports scheduled by the head of Athletics, in early years often between two groups while the whole camp watched, but later usually involving all cabins in pairs playing against each other on the many fields and courts. The staff expected that good sportsmanship would be developed in inter-cabin tournaments in all the competitive sports. From the beginning, one of these sports was softball, such a predominant enthusiasm in the first years of camp. Volleyball was not very satisfactory since rules were adapted to allow all cabinmates to be on the court at once. Girls ran their hearts out in field hockey and soccer. Some other less well-known games were deck tennis and Newcomb. Both games were played over a volleyball net, deck tennis with a ring and Newcomb with a ball like a volleyball, thrown back and forth over the net. (Deck tennis was played in the early 20th century on big cruise liners, and Newcomb was invented in 1895 by Clara Gregory Baer at Sophie Newcomb College in New Orleans.) At the turn of the

98

20th century, basketball and Newcomb were the first team games that women could play.[34] Deck tennis and Newcomb were perfect for young campers, developing eye-hand coordination, team play, and respect for game rules.

The volleyball (deck tennis and Newcomb) court was located between Senior Unit and the Rat Trap. Hockey and soccer were played on a field between the Chicken Coop and the fields near the outside road. There were also tennis and Ping-Pong, the latter played in the Korn Kribbe.

Vespers

After Tournaments and a stop at the drinking fountain, hot sweaty campers went back to the cabins to put on boots once again for Vespers. The counselor had a poncho to spread over the damp ground, and sometimes campers had one to contribute for the cabin. Dutch Logan describes it:

> By cabin groups we passed between Senior 2 and 3. We were to be silent and in a spirit of reverence. Vespers was held in a beautiful setting between two rows of evergreens, facing a birch cross and stone altar. We sang and worshiped. A visiting ordained pastor or student pastor always led the service.

Another camper, Martha McGonigle Mewhort says, "I think about rubber boots, sit upons, and walking beside friends to the outdoor chapel." Favorite hymns all had to do with nature in some way.

Favorite Vespers Hymns
God who touches earth with beauty
Day is dying in the west
Abide with me
This is my father's world
Now the day is over
For the beauty of the earth
Fairest Lord Jesus
(also known as *Beautiful Savior*)

Indeed, the outdoor chapel was a beautiful place, simple, peaceful, dear to Hagan campers' hearts no matter what denomination they came from or religious direction they might take as adults. The birch cross was first lodged in stones brought up by campers, year by year, from the shore of the river.[35] Later, in 1952, the stones were mortared in, the cement cross firmly embedded at the top.[36] Campers understood that it was more permanent but missed the rustic birch cross set in the pile of river rocks.

Birch cross in river rock

100

Entertainment

Where else could I have learned how to make
a wedding dress out of newspaper?
Linda Brandt Barr

Newspaper Costumes

In contrast to the competition of tournaments, entertainment gave campers an opportunity to share talents with each other and to laugh. There was entertainment every night. Of course, just about everything during the day was social, and usually entertaining, with campers working, learning, and playing together. But the evening entertainment was almost entirely devoted to socially broadening campers' lives in a simple, homespun way, mainly using materials at hand and creating entertainment together.

Korn Kribbe

Campers came to most entertainments, known in the *Memory Books* as "Evening Program," first in Great Hall in the '40s, then in the Korn Kribbe recreation hall, built in 1952. Very occasionally, campers watched performers from outside, such as a glassblower who came and demonstrated how to blow glass into little animal figures. But mainly campers were an audience for people they knew – CIT and JC shows, counselor shows or "Follies," Miller shows, talent shows, and amateur night. In 1956, the CITs performed *Peter Pan*, lip-synching the lyrics to a record of the popular musical. Nancy Engel was Peter Pan and Robin Fidler, head of CITs, played Tinker Bell. But far and away, the majority of entertainments consisted of cabin groups or, sometimes, mixes of juniors and intermediates with senior campers, making up skits. Typical activities were making things from objects in a bag, everyone born in the same month acting out a little skit, making costumes out of newspaper. There were scavenger hunts and treasure hunts, unit night and cabin night, talent shows (Amateur Night), sing-alongs, and Carnival Night (each cabin had a carney act or booth). Imagine a Kentoady Derby – yes, a toad race. Capture the Flag was always fun in the dark. Cabins also prepared skits for contests.

Some of these events were mildly competitive, but nobody thought much about it the next day, except perhaps winning song contests – that was always a thrill. Once a year, cabin groups wrote songs, usually changing words to current popular songs, which they sang for the Song Contest. Winning songs from each unit were printed in the next day's news sheets, *The Queue* or *Hagan Herald,* and some of them made their way into the Hagan songbook.

Entertainments drew on musical, dramatic, athletic, and creative talents, and, above all, continued the powerful social lesson of camp – working and playing together.

On the way back to the cabins after Entertainment campers sang:

> Now run along home, and jump into bed,
>
> Say your prayers and cover your head.
>
> The very same thing I say unto you,
>
> You dream of me and I'll dream of you.

On some Sunday nights, the Entertainment was called Unit Night, replacing the earlier Campers' Own. One night seniors had a contest painting faces on knees. At Cabin Night two cabins often sat together around fire rings between the cabins, with s'mores for treats. And, of course, ghost stories. One story about Bloody Mary and Hitler's Tomb, up on the hill (campers called it a mountain) across the road from camp, had a character probably named for Bloody Mary, Queen of Scots, in English history. Though almost everyone remembers Bloody Mary, no one remembers the actual story.

Cabin Devotions

The day closed with Cabin Devotions. Besides filling the religious purpose of meditative discussion of the Vespers service and personal reflections on the day, Cabin Devotions provided, as well, a time for busy, tired campers to wind down and get sleepy. Most recall Cabin Devotions fondly.

Taps

Taps was a sign for silence and lights out. Carol Jones Fuller, bugler from 1943 to 1947, remembers the thrill of walking alone up to the Rat Trap (administration building) at night to blow Taps under a beautiful starry sky. A decade later, Robin Fidler Brancato had the same experience, which she describes in the same words. All campers recall Taps as a beautiful time, a haunting sound, with everyone quiet and reverent.

> *[I also] remember sometimes failing to hit the high note.*
> Robin Fidler Brancato

Tired from all the day's activities, with Taps echoing in the night, Hagan campers slept well.

Endnotes

[33] The Buildings and Repairs report says 1959, but it seems to have been compiled some years later, from memory, not records.

[34] http://en.wikipedia.org/wiki/Newcomb_ball

[35] Mary Westhuis, '60s camper/counselor: My mom told me that the founding staff members contributed a rock to the altar. Jane Grigger says she heard from Janet Brookes (both '60s) that her mother helped build the altar in the late 40s. Stefanie MacAdam, Martha McGonigle Mewhort and I (author) remember the altar as a pile of rocks that we all brought up from the river each day.

[36] *Morning Watch* 1952

Interlude 1

Wildlife

One hot afternon, we had to "weed" the tennis court. Turned out it was full of bees' nests in the clay. Not a very good activity!
Jane Detwiler LeVan

We [counselors] had spent until 3 AM in Great Hall making things special for our campers at Hagan Christmas. Walking back to our cabins, exhausted and hands full, we crossed the path of a skunk. He was about a foot from us. The last thing we wanted was to get sprayed so we danced backward and plotted a new route to the cabins. The next day we laughed.
Letty Townsend Chadwick

Ruth Clegg Whitsel collected baby toads. The kitchen boys gave her a huge pickle jar, in which she planted moss and ferns, adding a small smooth river rock and a turned up lid filled with water for a pond. Feeding them was a cold-blooded affair: ants for everyday, flies with a wing removed for special treats. They even ate earthworms, a process that took about an hour. Here is her appreciation:

Ode to a Toad

Oh tiny speckled creature
With the Mona Lisa smile,
Whither goest thou,
Hopping through thy
Miniature green jungle?
If I please to pick thee up,
Thou wilt, no doubt,
Leave wet upon my hand.
No matter, I will love thee still.

106

If perchance I feed and house thee,
Canst thou love me back?

On an overnight hike we told everyone not to put any food, especially candy, in their sleeping bags. When the campers were all asleep and the counselors were sitting around the campfire, we saw a sudden movement in the bottom of a girl's sleeping bag and knew immediately what it was. We very carefully started lifting the sleeping bag from the bottom until the friendly little skunk crawled out right past her head. Skunk sashayed away and all was well, but we all breathed a sigh of relief and she never woke up.

Midge Wilkinson Vansant

Funniest thing: Ginny Davis skinning a snake

Inge Woerman Coleman

I was sitting on the grass during religion class, leaning against a tree. A small snake (a garter snake?) crawled up my back under my uniform shirt.

Gay Staudenmaier Moceri

One summer there was a huge commotion behind the senior cabins. Many campers were watching, screaming and running away from something. When I arrived I saw a 3 ft. black snake. I pinned it down with a forked stick, and picked it up by the head. The campers were in awe as they watched me carry it. I felt briefly like a local heroine.

Ruth Clegg Whitsel

In 1950 or thereabouts, skunks were everywhere and some nights I had to crawl out the window because there was one on the edge of the porch.

Midge Wilkinson Vansant

[In 1969 or 70] I took my cabin on an overnight to Bear Creek. After setting up camp, we went exploring and swam in the waterfall. When we came back to camp, our supply tent had been slashed and torn, a huge rip down the side of the tent. Some of our dehydrated food packs were missing. The campers blamed it on a raccoon. But we knew different! A raccoon can open a zipper. Our tent had been attacked by a bear. Not a very comfortable feeling for the night. No cell phones in those days!

Gay Staudenmaier Moceri

One day while we were living in the tents, Connie Kline put her hand in a coat pocket and discovered a family of baby mice!

Chris Hill Killough

A skunk was in the trash box in Dusty Glasson's junior cabin as her kids slept. She was terrified and left the cabin with sleeping campers to report it to all of us lounging in the Shack. I just recall eating watermelon and laughing our heads off as she told us.

Ruth Clegg Whitsel

I was playing field hockey when the counselor told us all to lie down on the grass. We did, and when we looked up, there was a beautiful eagle just soaring above us.

Gay Staudenmaier Moceri

"Skunks a guest at overnight hikes to Mini."
Hagan Herald Aug 5, 1943

Frogs seemed to be everywhere and I started making friends with them. The girls loved to see me pick up frogs and toads and kiss them. UUEWWW they'd scream. I got to be known as the frog lady and that is when people started giving me frog "things." I lived in Vermont with my own pond, where I raised my own frogs, and continued as a teacher to use frogs in my classroom.

Jane Billing Terry
108

I remember uncovering mouse nests complete with babies in mattresses when opening up camp for the season.
Phyllis Kaspareit Davidson

Late one night we awoke to our cabin counselor freaking out over a mouse. I saw it scurry up the shutter rope. Our cots alternated head to toe, and my good friend, sleeping next to me, turned so that her head was down at the aisle, like mine, and we squealed and shivered in fright. Huddled close together, it never occurred to us that the little creature was more afraid of us than we were of him.
Ruth Clegg Whitsel

The Skunk Song
The stars at night go twink-a-link-a-link
Away up in the sky,
The moon at night goes blink-a-link-a-link
It shines right in my eye.
The skunks at night go stink-a-link-a-link
I wish that they would die!
Oh, twink-a-link-a-link
Oh, blink-a-link-a-link
Oh, stink-a-link-a-link
Oh my!

Chapter 8

A Few of Our Favorite Things

Besides the daily schedule, what happened each week, each two-week camping period, and each summer?

Every Wednesday was Letter Home night, when campers had to bring a letter to parents as their meal ticket. Emma Hallman Mele says, "Believe me, it was a very short letter." Early on, the envelopes were to be left unsealed, probably to make sure there was actually something inside. But that must have gotten old fast – who wanted to check and then seal all those letters? Thus it was that Carolyn McGonigle Holleran, like others, got away with snatching a piece of toilet paper and writing "Gotta go!" to get to dinner in time. Campers had other strategies, too, to cope with the letter home requirement. An early camper, Betty Stefani Macadam, came to camp with "all my letters written from home to home. Unfortunately, my mother found the letters and they were destroyed PDQ. I thought it was a good idea 'cause that way I would not have lost Hagan time doing the boring letter writing."

The letter home was more than a meal ticket – it was a ticket for the Wednesday night movie, which nobody wanted to miss. At first the movies were shown in Great Hall, then in the Korn Kribbe (recreation hall), built in 1952. The golden age of movies, from the end of the silent era in the 1920s to the early '60s, made for good watching. Movies were generally shown two or three years after they opened and had their run in

> Movie Memories
> Abbot and Costello
> *The Jungle Book*
> Shirley Temple
> *The Master of Ballantrae*
> (Errol Flynn)
> *Mr. Smith goes to Washington* (Jimmy Stewart)
> *Goodbye Mr. Chips*
> Esther Williams water pageants
> Bob Hope and Dorothy Lamour road trips
> Sonja Henie ice skating
> *Charlie McCarthy, Detective* (Edgar Bergen, ventriloquist)

110

first- and second-tier theaters. And then shown again, and again. Campers were still watching the 1936 *Pennies from Heaven* with Bing Crosby.

The Phantom of the Opera had a colorful history at Hagan. The first time it was shown, the little ones got so frightened their counselors had to take them out in the middle. Early Hagan campers saw *Phantom* in the original silent version with Lon Chaney and later in the 1943 version with Claude Rains. Emma Hallman Meles says, "Scary!! We walked back to our cabin holding onto each other." It became a staple, and for many Hagan alums, *Phantom* is the only movie they remember.

On scrub day, every Friday morning, the beds from all cabins were carried out, buckets of water lugged from the shower house, and cabin floors scrubbed with brooms. This was bedsheet-changing time, too, putting the top sheet on the bottom, sending the bottom sheet to the laundry, and laying a clean sheet on top. Then, of course, the blankets were added to make a Hagan-style bed. Friday mornings also brought hairwash – in the river. This was actually fun, though probably not great

> *Someone left a box of records out in the sun while cleaning cabins –*
> *the records melted together.*
> Jane Detwiler LeVan

for the river ecology. Counselors or CITs checked as girls came out of the water to make sure all the soap was out of their hair.

Yet another regular event for Friday mornings was swim tests. Swimming was big at Camp Hagan. Because the swim cap color changed with the swim level achieved, according to Red Cross standards, getting to the next level was especially exciting. The campus newssheet *The Queue* reports on August 30, 1941, that "in spite of the icy water, there were many girls who stayed down to finish up their tests." Girls working toward the highest level of swimming had the opportunity – and thrill – on a few occasions of swimming across the river for their half-hour swim (without getting out of the water on the Jersey side).

The final weekly event was Sunday church service. The pastor for the week conducted the service with the assistance of the Religion counselor. Interested campers, especially those working on requirements for their tie awards, participated. Girls sat on long low uncomfortable benches in the Korn Kribbe. An altar was set up and Lutheran liturgy was followed. Sometimes there was a choir. It was often very hot, and for some girls it was the least favorite time of week. For others, the familiar service and the uplifting hymns were satisfying. Some girls preferred their religion out in the Vespers chapel, where they felt closer to nature.

Change Days and Visiting Days

In 1939 the promotional brochure tells parents, "We must insist on visiting days – Saturday and Sunday ONLY," which suggests that in the very first couple of years visiting may have been somewhat random, even chaotic. In 1943 the hours from 2:00-5:00 on weekend days were specified. Of campers from this period, no one can figure out how Hagan managed visitors in the midst of Special Days, which took place on odd-numbered Saturdays, but it continued for a surprising number of years. By 1955 someone in administration must have said "Enough!" and visiting days were only at Change Day weekends, no others.

Special Days

On alternate Saturdays, in between change days, Hagan campers loved Special Days. Many were constructed so that girls from different age groups – junior, intermediate, and senior – could work together on teams that cut across cabin and unit lines. This arrangement gave younger campers opportunities to work and play alongside older campers as their models and older campers a chance to learn patience and kindness with younger ones. Campers got especially involved in Hagan Olympics, when six teams representing six countries vied for championships in track and field events. (Brooms over chairs served as hurdles.) Campers competed for their "countries" in high jump, broad jump, and relays. It was an honor to be chosen a team captain. Some camps had color wars all season long, where cabins were assigned a color from the very beginning, which must have made for deeply held, summer-long competitive feelings. But Hagan's system encouraged cooperation within intense competition, which, after a rousing game of Capture the Flag, ended at the end of the day.

Wheelbarrows used for Special Day games

Laurel Wreath Olympics Winner, 1951

Another favorite was Army-Navy Day, complete with campers wearing red and blue colors, a football game finale, and a Navy sailor and a two-person Army mule. There was also a Hagan Circus, held in the spacious parking lot between Great Hall and the outside road. Christine Hill Killough's

Cheerleaders on Army-Navy Day

family made home movies of that day, probably in 1940, that show her sister as "the painted lady with lipstick and stickers of some kind all over her." The Associate Director, Mac (Kathryn Reinbold) was the ring master. These, along with the Space Spree, show topics for Special Days being drawn from existing interests in the broader society. A continuing influence of the native-American theme in camping appears in the Shawnee Powwow Special Day. Billhilly Day suggests that Hagan was no more culturally sensitive than most of the rest of mainstream America.

Campfire

> *Round about the council fire bright*
> *We have come in comradeship tonight.*
> *Round about the whispering trees*
> *Guard our Hagan memories...*
> Favorite campfire song, to the tune of
> *Til We Meet Again*[37]

Campfires were held Friday night at the end of each two-week session. On the way to campfire, called Council Fire, campers in their cabin groups passed the totem pole, a present made by Camp Miller and given to Hagan in 1949, according to Bep Berger. The big campfire circle was ringed by pines. For several years new trees were dedicated at campfire to a country in the Olympics. As at Vespers, campers sat on ponchos. The Pioneering department had already built the campfire itself, in the center, with a tipi of kindling branches inside a log cabin of big logs. The campers sang *Kneel Always When You Light a Fire*, and camper torchbearers came in from north, east, south, and west, referencing native Americans' offering of morning prayers to the four winds, with torches made from gauze soaked in melted paraffin at the end of long straight branches. The torchbearers each made a little dedication, for example, "With this torch I light the fire of service, service to camp, to country, and service to God. Help us, Lord, to keep our fire of fellowship, leadership, character, and service burning."

Campfire was a time of songs, stories, and awards, a mixture of reverence and fun. Most of these had beautiful harmonies, and many girls improvised these. Rounds, like *White Coral Bells*, worked well around the campfire, and even girls who felt they couldn't sing well participated happily within the support of their group. The camp director or a designated song leader made sure songs started at a singable pitch and kept together. Camp Hagan seemed to bring out the music in everybody.

Favorite Campfire Songs
Father Time
Jacob's Ladder
Tell Me Why
From the Mountains Here at Hagan (to the tune of The Whiffenpoof Song (Yale 1907)
Drifting and Dreaming (1925)
If There Were Witchcraft
Each Campfire Burns Anew
Round About the Council Fire Bright

The story of Haga-Ann was told once each month. This tale is a very old legend, appearing in many parts of the country, especially the eastern part. In Kit Berger's words, preserved in the Hagan Scrapbook/Wooden Album from 1949, the story and its meaning:

115

There's a spirit among us which comes from the long ago when an Indian maiden and a pioneer child met in our hills, yes, perhaps here at this very spot. The legend tells us that Haga, the Indian girl, found Ann hurt and sick and lost. Haga opened her heart to her. For long days she tenderly cared for her new friend until she became well and strong. When it was time for her new friend to return to her home, she couldn't bear the thought of parting, so they pledged each other to stay together the rest of their days. That, so the legend goes, is how the spirit of Hagan – which means friendship – came to be. If we would have friends, we must be friendly.

We know, of course, that Hagan doesn't really mean friendship; it's a man's name. And how the two girls would have managed to stay together for the rest of their lives is not part of the story. But this legend tells us that both the lesson of friendship and the continuance of Indian themes were important to Camp Hagan.

Awards were given out at campfire for swim tests, ties, Honor Council, and Best All-round Camper, announced by the Associate Director. New Honor Council members were tapped by current members, walking around behind the circle until they stopped at the surprised girls and brought them to the center when their names were read aloud.

In the early years Mac (Ruth McLaughlin), an Aquatics counselor, told "star stories," so star-gazing was for a while a campfire feature.

At the end of campfire, campers and counselors formed a friendship circle (right arm crossed over left, holding hands with girls on either side) and sang "Blest Be the Tie That Binds." They left the campfire circle singing "To the Knights in the Days of Old (Follow the Gleam)."

If campfire was rained out, the event was held in the Korn Kribbe (or earlier, in Great Hall). Indoors was a sad substitute for the campfire circle. In 1950 it rained every campfire but the last one, according to the *Hagan Herald,* and we don't know for sure that it didn't for the last.

Of course the 4th of July was a yearly event, celebrated with fireworks, on whatever day of the week the 4th fell. But some special events occurred one time only, such as the hike into Bushkill to see an actual circus, with many trips by the truck to get campers home after dark. The Juniors had a hay ride – that was fun.

Campers also signed up for playdays with other nearby camps, such as Indian Lake, Camp Akiba, Hugh Beaver (a Y camp), Pocono Highlands Camp, and Paradise Falls, who all shared with Hagan that swatch of the Poconos. Volleyball and softball were the main events. Teams were often mixed, making the fun of the play more important than the competition between camps. Girls rode in the camp truck singing "Everybody take your hats off to Hagan," "We are the Hagan girls," and "Ei-Yi-Ki-Yi-Kus, nobody like us, we are the girls from Camp Hagan."

There were two twice yearly summer events, one the Hagan-Miller Dance and the other taking camp pictures. The Hagan-Miller dance was held in one month at Camp Hagan and the other month at Camp Miller. Girls wore dresses or skirts and helped each other with their hair. Boys, it was said, practiced dancing. Dances held at Hagan were in Great Hall in the early years and then in the '50s in the Korn Kribbe. These settings were decorated with a theme such as "Undersea Wonderland." In 1949 in Great Hall, the theme was "Campus Kapers," with pennants from many East Coast colleges. Perhaps this reflects not so much the aspirations of campers as the experience and interests of the counseling and administrative staff. Although some campers would rather have been nearly anywhere else, most senior campers looked forward to the dances. The camp truck made many trips delivering and retrieving Miller Mugs and Hagan Hags.

Camp pictures were taken in the second and fourth sessions. These are wonderful old pictures, about five inches by twelve, with five or six long rows of campers, littlest ones in front, counselors in the top row. There were also pictures of staff members making faces and trying silly poses, very goofy. Unfortunately, campers and counselors were not identified. How we wish they had been!

Camp Picture, 1941

Camp Picture, 1951

Totem Pole, 1950

May Day was a popular yearly special event, occurring on the third Friday in July. A queen and court were elected by all campers, and although the queen and maids were indeed very pretty, this event was far from The Miss America pageants that were also hugely popular at that mid-century time. Hagan's May Day was a re-enactment of real or imagined

Some May Queens
Carol Jones
Alice Bomberger
Helga Hagadorn
Jinx Jinsura
Trudy Hagedorn
Inge Woermann
Nancy Kelly

old English country May Day celebrations, featuring parades, May Pole dances with ribbons, jesters, and perhaps a play – in 1950, "Hansel and Gretel." Though in the first years May Day was held on the green around the flag pole, the remainder were held in the outdoor theater and are recorded in many campers' photo albums across the years.

Once a year all the campers wrote on a ballot their candidates for the

May Day Mural

119

Hagan Popularity Contest. Most Popular was only the third item on the list. First was the Funniest. The list also included Quietest, Biggest Feet, Peppiest, Longest Legs, and Most Cheerful, among others. Nobody was known to be miffed if she wasn't chosen Most Popular, let alone Biggest Eater or Biggest Pest.

Amid regular, well-organized happenings, Haganites also learned to cope with the unexpected. Certainly weather provided many unscheduled events at Hagan. Thunderstorms were frequent, and one night in 1941 *The Queue* reported a "rip-snortin' storm," as thunder and lightning rolled around the Poconos. Pat Fletcher recalls a summer of heavy rains when "they opened the flood gates up-river from Hagan and just about wiped out our waterfront."

Pranks and misbehavior also occurred irregularly. Carol Jones Fuller reports at night putting a bucket of water on top of the cabin door, "then making noise so the counselor on duty would come and get doused." Bep Berger says waterfront counselors had a big surprise when Miller painted the inside of the rowboats blue. Once camp awoke to see paint on the Great Hall roof, another stealthy application by Camp Miller. Sometimes pajamas or a bra would appear in the morning at the top of the flagpole. One camper in the '50s received some underwear in the mail at real Christmastime. That mystery remained unsolved.

Short-sheeting someone's bed, often the counselor's, was indulged. Pie beds were thankfully less common (Ch. 4). "Cutting up," making noise after Taps, was more risky – unit heads didn't find it funny, and some counselors felt insulted that their cabin was misbehaving. But this transgression was fun, talking and singing in the dark into an otherwise silent night.

For most campers, the absolute favorite event of the summer was Hagan Christmas. Dutch Logan says she signed up for the last two weeks to be there for that celebration. Research has not revealed any other Christian camps where the holiday was enacted as it was at Camp Hagan. Beginning in the last two-week session, campers were urged to make their Christmas gifts for the cabinmate whose name they drew, called the

Pollyanna exchange. The many reminders in the camp news sheets, *The Queue* and the *Hagan Herald,* sound like contemporary advertisements: "Only *x* number of shopping days until Christmas!" Everybody exchanged Christmas cards – last year's, brought from home, with any names or notes cut off. Experienced campers brought their own and their parents', and counselors brought extras, so there were plenty to go around. Also, throughout the week campers sang Christmas carols. By the end of August when Hagan Christmas arrived, singing was second nature to most everyone, and all seemed to enjoy the old carols as well as some popular songs such as "White Christmas" and "Rudolph."

On Christmas Eve, campers hung their stockings or placed them around the big fireplace in Great Hall. Decorations were up and the youngest camper lit the bayberry candle while everyone made a wish.

On Christmas morning, always held on Thursday, campers went to

breakfast in their pajamas (and boots – it was unfailingly wet in the mornings). They did the Hokey Pokey and snake-danced around the flagpole singing – in the '50s, "Here We Go Loop Dee Loo," a song which somehow had made its way from a 1950 British

Christmas Morning

TV show to Camp Hagan. Stockings, filled by the counselors the night before, contained an orange, Christmas cards, and the Pollyanna gift from the cabinmate in the name-draw. In the early years, a lump of coal was in there, too. The rest of the day was a play day, with games and activities around the campus.

Christmas banquet was an actual turkey dinner, with all the fixin's. Great Hall was decorated with greens and handmade decorations, usually done by the seniors, and at each dinner place was a program with the menu and the evening's schedule of events. The new mural was unveiled, joining the much-loved others on the walls.

Miller and Hagan exchanged Christmas gifts. In 1941 Miller's gift to Camp Hagan was a Christmas wreath.

Sometimes campers or CITs presented a play or pageant, for example *The Birds' Christmas Carol*. Trios or groups of campers also performed popular songs such as "Winter Wonderland," and CITs sang "Twas the Night Before Christmas."

Awards were given out at the banquet. Besides the regular two-weeks' awards, other ties that took longer to earn or the silver acorn that could take two years to complete were bestowed, as well as Best All-Round Camper for the year.

And the Yule log saved from the previous year's banquet was added to the fire in the big fireplace at one end of Great Hall.

The Last Campfire

Friday of the last week was spent scrubbing the cabins once more, packing, and generally lounging around in a way that was never permitted during the summer session. The last night of camp saw the whole camp gathered around the council fire circle. Kit (Kathryn Berger) wrote amazing pieces for the last campfire each year, 1948 - 1952. She detailed the past summer's activities in "The Year That Was," and, with gentle humor in "The Year That Would Never Come," predicted all the wonderful or unlikely things that the future might hold for staff and well-known campers. It went on for pages. In rhyme! These carefully scripted programs were saved in the *Hagan Scrapbook* (*Wooden Album*). Campfire songs were interspersed, with "Jacob's Ladder" a favorite.

> *One year Meg Brown Papa, Sue Carmint Knorr and I sang at the top of the steps the same three songs, over and over – "Prayer" from Hansel and Gretel, "You'll Never Walk Alone," and "One Little Candle."*
> Alice

Campers and counselors left the Council Fire Circle singing "To the Knights in the Days of Old" and then filed down the steps to the river for the candle float. Usually the Aquatic Club sang down on the beach.[38]

Campers lit their little candles from a counselor's larger candle, dripped the wax so that the candle would stand firm on the small squares of balsa wood, made a wish, and pushed them out into the river. For campers and counselors it was magical, but in later years some have wondered if, downriver the next morning, people were saying, "Here come those darn candles again!"

At breakfast on the last morning, counselors gathered in a circle in front of the big stone fireplace in Great Hall, arms around each other's shoulders, and sang "Bless 'Em All," another old song from pre-World War I:

Bless 'em all, bless 'em all,
The long and the short and the tall.
Bless all the campers who play hard all day,
Bless all the counselors who tuck them away.
For we're saying good-bye to them all
As back to the city they go.
There'll be no Camp Hagan until the next season,
So cheer up my girls, bless 'em all.[39]

Going home was for many girls a tearful time, often to the bewilderment of their parents. Why should their daughters not want to go home? Sometimes the cause was fear of starting junior or senior high school, or perhaps a new school, or facing other home problems. But generally it was the sadness of leaving friends, the outdoors, the comforting pattern of the days, the learning and playing and doing. The *Hagan Herald*, August 21, 1952, bid campers farewell as they went "back to the crowded cities," one of the earliest themes of camping.

Endnotes

---

[37] World War I song, 1918, by Richard Whiting

[38] *One Little Candle* was popular after 1945 when it was the theme song of a television program known as "The Christophers." The idea of the song derived originally from an ancient Chinese proverb, "It's better to light a candle than to curse the darkness."]

[39] "Bless Them All" was sung in the British army in the 1890s. It continued to be popular in WW I in Britain, sung by and for male audiences, and did not originally say *"Bless."* It was cleaned up for general audiences and became very popular as a singalong between the wars and on into WW II. http://www.fredgodfreysongs.ca/Songs/Bless_em_all.htm]

Chapter 9

There's a Place That's Meant
for You and Me[40]

Loved earning all the color ties.
Anita Zimmerly

What Awards Did Campers Earn?

Earning awards and honors contributed to the formation of campers and the women they would become. Awards were important – but not overly so. Girls were proud to earn ties, but nobody looked down on anyone who wasn't working for one. Girls who earned them one year always wore them the next year, but most campers of the 1940s and '50s agree that girls who didn't earn ties weren't stigmatized. An early camper, Chris Hill Killough, says she was "not a tie-person because I could not swim! I didn't feel left out at all."

From the camp administration's point of view, awards showed results of the experiences and skills the camp offered. Awardees got to do things in every department and accomplish things they didn't know they could.

Ties

In the early '40s, there were two Junior Camp (Juniors and Intermediates) awards, called "Crickets," or Red Tie, and "Whippoorwills," or Green Tie, and two Senior Camp awards, "Rangers," or Blue Tie, and "Prospectors," the White Tie. (Note the connection to nature with whippoorwills and to pioneering with prospectors.) The requirements at first were presented in the *Memory Books* in four categories: Physical, Educational, Social, and Moral. From 1944 to 1950, no awards were mentioned at all (except for horsemanship in '44).

After 1950 the criteria for the ties were listed in the *Memory Books*. As they were completed, the head of each department signed in a column labeled "Passed by" to signify completion of that set of requirements.

By 1950 the "Crickets" and "Whippoorwills" had become the Red Chevron for Juniors and Intermediates and Blue Chevron for Seniors, both for two-week campers. The Green Tie and Yellow Tie were added for Juniors and Intermediates who were staying longer. In addition to the Blue and White Ties, no longer called the "Ranger" or "Prospector," there was a Silver Acorn Award, for which campers were allowed two years to complete. By 1953 the Junior Acorn for Juniors and Intermediates appeared. A "Specialization Award" was added in 1954 for seniors who had the silver acorn, an award that encouraged them to work and learn in the department of their choice. No particular requirements were listed; they were to be decided between the camper and the department head. The Specialization Award did not last long, in fact not many campers knew it was there, and in 1955 it was replaced with the Citizenship Award, based on "sportsmanship, leadership, cooperation, and character."

> *Ruth Clegg Whitsel and I did a radio play about an elderly couple talking, and frequently wondering about the noise they're hearing. It ended with "Listen! The gardener's boy is planting flowers on our grave!"*
> Alice

Also by the '50s the categories of requirements had changed to the three general goals of the Hagan motto: Socially Broaden, Physically Fortify, and Spiritually Deepen. Under "Socially Broaden," Camp Citizenship came first and was the same for all awards: "A camper must display a spirit of cooperation and sportsmanship in all activities, whether it be in a cabin group, a unit, or camp program as a whole."

Arts and Crafts were seen as socially broadening: work on the mural, make things in ceramics, wood, and leather, and exhibiting one's work. Entertainment also provided socially broadening experiences: singing in Vespers Choir or participating in Entertainment classes or programs.

The goal of "Physically Fortify" was met in the departments of

Athletics, Aquatics, Pioneering, Nature, and Health. Campers were expected to spend a certain number of instructional hours in sports, learn rules of games they chose, pass certain levels of swim tests, learn how to build a campfire, make a bedroll (yes, still), identify trees and plants, and know how to use a First Aid kit.

> *I had to preach a little sermon at a vesper*
> *service as a CIT. I remember it well.*
> Posie Bosek Clymer

For "Spiritually Deepen," campers were to take part in one or more Vespers services and offer a prayer or thought in Cabin Devotions. Campers who worked to earn the silver acorn found especially memorable the requirement to give a sermon at Vespers. Scary, but exciting and satisfying.

Honor Council and Best All-around Camper

> *I think there were many accomplishments and*
> *I seemed to be unaware of most of them at the time.*
> Phyl Kaspareit Davidson

Another kind of award looked to a different facet of camp life, something we might call "campership" (though that word was not used) – Honor Council and Best All-around Camper. These awards were an expansion of, or focus on, the qualities for camp citizenship required for all the ties. Honor Council provided the Honor Guard at Flag Raising and Torch-bearers at Campfire, and at the end of the year they went on a picnic to someplace like Child's Park.

Of course, for any award that does not have specific check-off criteria, subjectivity inevitably intrudes. Campers who were selected for Honor Council and Best All-around Camper were to some extent the ones the counselors and administrative staff liked best. But experience suggests that these girls really were good campers. Girls who were not chosen usually looked at the recipients with admiration and some longing.

Rewards of Returning

Loved it, loved everything, loved the camp life.
The sentiment of several campers

The many campers who attended for several years, often going on to become counselors, are a small group of the whole of Hagan family. Those who contributed to this book were among those who loved it, but there are hundreds and hundreds of campers who were perhaps "one and done" attendees. We do not know why these campers didn't return – other enticing opportunities, family plans or needs, or disaffection, disinterest.

Not everyone would have loved Camp Hagan, or camp at all. But for those who did and returned for many years, often for ten or more, Hagan was a happy place that played a formative role in their lives. Rosie Hallman Steen probably spent the most years at camp, from age six to nineteen, in all, fourteen years – a lot of love and loyalty.

The answers to why campers came back to Hagan comes from responses to questionnaires sent to former campers (See App. 4). There is great unanimity in these responses, with a few simple themes. By far the most common responses are "I loved it" and "I was happy there."

One recurring theme is accomplishment in activities, adventures, and challenges. As Jan Mueller describes it, "Canoe trips, hikes to Hidden Lake, being able to try new sports ... all activities on the waterfront, even carrying the canoes up the hill when the Delaware flooded."

Some campers had a brother at Miller, so that was a bonus to "loved it."

Many came back as counselors as long as they could afford it. It didn't pay very much, but for Phyllis Wiest Gilbert it was a "fun summer job." Campers generally found the counselors, indeed the whole environment, to be nurturing. One camper reported having gone to a more upscale camp and preferring the simplicity that characterized Camp Hagan.

And always, there were the friends, the connection with other girls, the formation of strong bonds that in some cases would last a lifetime. This was especially important in a time when the disparity between men's and women's lives and opportunities were starting to become recognized. The bonds among women were tight in earlier gender-segregated society, but social structures affirming the value of girls' and women's bonds with each other were not yet in place. Campers who were only children loved "being with all the kids." For all, campers and counselors alike, Camp Hagan was the bedrock for sisterly relationships, emotional connections, and support.

Along with loving it, campers and counselors speak of being happy at Hagan. Security and comfort were the underpinnings to the attitude of "I can do this." Some insightful girls knew that in this place they could become the person they strove to be. Many camper/counselors attest to the "spirit" of Hagan, made up of all these qualities. It was, finally, a wonderful way to spend the summer.

The surroundings contributed greatly to campers' pleasure in being at Camp Hagan.

When I started there, I was living in the city... el trains; untended vacant lots; street trash; supermarkets; movie theaters; trash trucks; cars; trolleys; coal bins/trucks; street people; and what I considered big ugly, trashy sycamores along the curb. Lots of cement. Not a lot of really fresh air.
Ruth Clegg Whitsel

Especially the river, but also the hills and trees, took on almost mystical properties, feeding a need voiced by the earliest camp founders – to live close to nature – at least as close as could be safely reconstructed for youngsters.

And laughter. Whatever else was going on in their lives away from camp, girls were safe and happy at Hagan, free to laugh and laugh, often having no idea what started the giggles and peals of laughter.

Why did campers/counselors leave?

There were tearful goodbyes on the last day of camp, and that was just the end of one summer. Imagine then the sadness, the emotional rupture that campers and counselors felt at leaving permanently this place where they had done much of their growing up.

Everyone knew that no matter how many summers spent at camp, it would come to an end for each camper personally. Counselors whom longtime campers had watched grow up from seniors to CITs and counselors, even department heads, were there – and then they weren't. Those who became department heads and even directors, it was felt, were inestimably fortunate. For some, painfully, not being asked back as counselor or in the CIT/JC program resulted in their departure.

Many left for summer jobs that would pay more. One left after her CIT year because her father felt she should get a real job. The need for better earnings drove many decisions not to return to Camp Hagan. Summer secretary was one sort of job, and for some few, there were better–paying jobs at other camps, usually drawing on expertise honed at Hagan. Some camper/counselors had begun full-time jobs and couldn't get the summer off.

For some, other interests took the place of camp. For example, one girl's father bought her a horse, and since horseback riding was her passion, there was just no contest (though she sent her daughter to Hagan years later). In another instance, a camper's Girl Scout troop developed international connections that drew her away.

Going to college marked the time for some to stop going to summer camp while for others that time came after a year or two into college. Summer school drew some away, either because of the need to make up credits or because of an opportunity to study abroad or in special programs. Then, too, family needs often had to be met, owing to illness or other situations.

And finally, for most young women, graduation, marriage and family, and serious jobs ensued – and the rest of life without camp. Most were realistic about the change: it was time. But this was, after all, where a wonderful part of growing up had taken place. Both campers and counselors were sad to lose the deep bonds of friendship that had been forged. Some felt bereft at the loss of something that had played such a big role in their lives, of summers spent living and learning with so many sisters.

And Then

After camp the other part of life took over. A large number of women reported marriage and being mothers first, and then entering the work force after their children were older. Those who worked while their children were smaller, out of choice or necessity, know how hard that was. These were women who grew up in the '40s and '50s, when the expectations for girls to marry and have children were shown in the pages of every *Ladies Home Journal* and at school, where girls took home economics and boys took shop. After WWII, men had come home and resumed jobs that women had been doing, and women were to return to home and hearth.

Many young women from Hagan went to college or other post-secondary education, most on the East Coast, and many, of course, in Pennsylvania (see App. 5). Some went back to school in their thirties to finish college or get advanced degrees, part of the first wave of women returning to college, an important milestone in the 20th century move toward equal education.

Many women who worked were unprepared to do so. We can be proud, even awed, for the women who raised their children as their primary work in life, a full-time job in itself, as well as those who ventured into the workplace, professions, and career – in those years, uncharted territory.

Did Hagan alums become stars? Not that we know of. But Hagan was never about that. Camp Hagan turned out girls and young women who became good people, kind, more or less cheerful, who were able to learn what they needed to learn when they needed to learn it.

Accomplishments and Life Lessons

I Can Row a Boat, Canoe?
(very) old joke[41]

Who knows when you might need to row a boat? In fact, many campers report boating, canoeing, and kayaking as pleasures throughout their lives, all based on what they learned on the waterfront at Camp Hagan. Many found their greatest accomplishment was teaching campers to swim, and one recalls helping to save a girl on waterfront who had an epileptic seizure.

Silver acorn campers remember giving the sermon in Vespers as their best thing. Being elected May Queen was special. For many, acceptance into the CIT program, or moving up from CIT to JC to cabin counselor, gave them pride, and especially being named department head. Not to mention becoming directress! Others felt their role as a counselor was their greatest success – being a friend to campers and growing up themselves.

> *My first Elderhostel was a canoe trip on the Delaware. We only went downstream from Dingman's Ferry to north of the Water Gap. At Hagan, we paddled up stream as well as down!*
> Phyl Kaspareit Davidson

And singing played its role, as in so many aspects of camp life. Some girls have said they rarely sang because they knew, had been told, they didn't have a good voice, but in singing with a whole camp around them, they learned to be at ease, comfortable.

Most campers said that the friendships made at Hagan taught them that they could, indeed, make friends, lifelong friends. Many still have friends from camp days.

Many girls who perhaps didn't shine at home or in school found at camp that they could be successful in activities that made them feel better, stronger in their own skin. For many campers, these provided their greatest achievements during those years. For those who were already successful in school, camp provided a whole different environment in which to grow, learn, and accomplish goals not available to them elsewhere.

Campers' accomplishments arise from the meshwork of activities, awards, and honors at Hagan. What people recall as their greatest achievement is a window to what they learned, a clue to life lessons. It is impossible to catalogue all that was learned. Here are just a few applications found in adult lives:

As mothers, former campers taught their children to swim. And to sing. Many campers have said they taught their children and grandchildren lots of camp songs, though Lyn Brandt Barr drew the line at "Mouse on the Barroom Floor."

Many still make square corners on beds (fitted bottom sheets and duvets have taken away the need for a lot of that) and place their towels folds to the door. They also report a low rate of success getting spouses or partners to do the folds-to-the-door thing.

Some have used what they learned in pioneering to make a fire (fortunately there's rarely a need to start a flame by twirling a stick in a hole in another stick to get a spark) and enjoyed camping with families and friends.

It's true: no one we know of went on to be an archery champion. But in sum, all the departments gave campers the opportunity to learn things they would not have been exposed to at home or in school.

In general, research in psychology shows that learning and pleasure are intertwined. When we learn, the pleasure part of our brain is stimulated along with whatever area is managing the incoming material that we're learning. Do children do well in school because they like it, or like it because they do well? Which naturally leads us to think of – archery! The first time of actually hitting the target was always a thrill. But as Hagan campers reveal over and over again, the usefulness of this kind of learning was not so much the skill acquired but the knowledge that you *could*. You could acquire new skills, understand a system, and accomplish a task with others working toward the same goal. For instance, making it through homesickness. Or hiking. The trek up to Hidden Lake (now known as Sunfish Pond) on the Appalachian trail is challenging, one that most people who did it never duplicated. But they know that they could and did.

> *One of my most fulfilling experiences was teaching my mother to swim the crawl. She could float on her back and do the sidestroke, but was afraid to put her face in the water. "One-two-three bubble bubble bubble."*
> Alice

Hagan campers didn't learn to live charmed lives where everything went right. There were the predictable mix of joyous and heartbreaking events in marriages, child-rearing, and careers, and the actuarial numbers of losses of family and beloved friends. But the goals stated in the Hagan motto – socially broaden, physically fortify, and spiritually deepen – took root and grew in later lives. What campers did take along: a strength and toughness, alums like to think, from the river, being able to feel at peace with nature, quiet and calm in natural surroundings, and the capacity to deal with a variety of disasters, like canoes overturning, poison ivy, the river on a rampage, hurricanes roaring in from the Atlantic. Those who remained in Lutheran or other churches found their faith deepened, expanded, more comprehensive. Some became unchurched in later life but continued to find their spiritual home in the hills, the woods, the river. All took the memory of the serene Vespers chapel with them, a place to go in the mind for solace and renewal.

And, finally, campers took the lessons of how to be friends, how to make friends, how to sustain friendships. These lessons and others echo in the pages of this book as we turn to the 1960s, the Last Generation, when '60s Haganites would build upon all that generations in the '30s, '40s, and '50s had done, writing their own lives into Hagan's history, before the Hagan-Miller merger to come.

Old Friends
From L to R, Top: Ruth Clegg Whitsel, Inge Woermann
Coleman,
Bottom: Phyllis Wiest Gilbert, Alice Royer Roy
(Taken by Pat Ulrich Ritter)

Endnotes

---

[40] Early Camp Hagan song. Didn't make it into the 1964 songbook.

[41] Al Jolson. *The Independent* June 17, 1916, v 35-36, p. 3. https://books.google.com/books?id=clRJAQAAMAAJ

Interlude 2

Canoe canoe?

About canoe trips, we remember the dangers, near catastrophes, and severe though temporary discomforts more than we do the highlights, the thrills, the beauties of our experiences. Besides, they make good stories. But you'd have to ask, if there so many awful events, why keep going on canoe trips? The thrill of running even the modest rapids of that stretch of the Delaware and the happiness felt cruising in the calm water out in the sunshine remained foremost, even if less often expressed. Here are some of Hagan camper/counselors' memories:

Weather turned real bad, stayed overnight on bank of rocks miles north of camp under canoes.
Carol Jones Fuller

The time I upset a canoe full of clothing coming home from an overnight.
Jane Detwiler LeVan

We paddled upriver as long as we could, but it was a flash flood and then we had to painfully walk the canoes against the current. We were walking along what had been a steep bank, hanging on to the canoes, stumbling over rocks, bushes, weeds, stumps. You couldn't see because the water was so muddy, including the poison ivy. We camped overnight in a field and phoned at a farm that we were safe.
Dutch (Dorothy) Dutcher

Falling out of canoe in rapids when bobbing on gunnels.
Anita Zimmerly Chaney

Worst: On a canoe trip from Dingman's Ferry, one canoe capsized on the way down and lost much of our food, which wasn't tied down
137

properly, and we were lucky that no one drowned.
Best: Canoeing across the Delaware at Miller to hike the Appalachian Trail to Hidden Lake (now Sunfish Pond), which was breathtaking and always my favorite.

Inge Woermann Coleman

On a trip to Kittatinny, one of the old brown canvas canoes hit a rock going through the rapids. It cracked the canoe. For the remainder of the trip, the person sitting in the middle did a lot of bailing!

Gay Staudenmaier Moceri

Canoe stress – carrying them up from the beach, maybe in the '55 flood.

Robin Fidler Brancato

I was trying to pass a canoeing test (for an award tie, I think), and the counselor in the canoe with me was Jeanie Worth. When I did the jump-overboard-then-get-back-in part of the test, I didn't do it right, and I dumped her in the water too! (I did eventually pass the test, though.)

Karen Blickwede Knowlton

Loved the canoe trips, bobbing (often falling in) and just generally being in the river. There was one rainy canoe trip up river where we spent the night under the overturned canoes to try to keep the worst of the downpour from hitting us directly.

Phyllis Kaspareit Davidson

I remember canoe trips as being the most fun part of Camp Hagan. I especially liked going through the rapids where I sat in the front of the canoe looking for big rocks and using the handle end of the paddle to repel the canoe away from a big rock when necessary. When I went to a Hagan reunion, I took a short canoe trip. No rapids, but it was fun to know that I hadn't forgotten how to canoe in over 60 years.

Pat Coffee

Sleeping in pouring rain on overnight canoe trips.
Lyn Brandt

Canoeing down from Dingman's Ferry, we camped at a landing near Bushkill. The next morning, when we packed up the canoes and slid softly into the water, it was still early but the mist had risen. The sun was shining, bringing with it some welcome warmth. Just ahead, after we launched, was a large bend in the river. This stretch was deep and calm and quiet. Some of the late summer leaves had begun to fall from the trees. A few were still green, others already turned to shades of gold. Scattered around us, they floated slowly along the surface of the tranquil water, at times gently swirling in the wake of our paddles. Sunlight glistened on the water and reflected off the leaves. No one spoke. Something magical had briefly settled there.
Ruth Clegg Whitsel

Part III: The End

1960s

Chapter 10

Hurricanes and Floods

"What was your greatest challenge as a director?"
"The hurricanes."
Jane Endres Hock, Director 1955 -1957

There were events in the camp year, and then there were *events*.
Hurricanes Connie and Diane, in 1955, and the ensuing floods, were
bigger events, with greater consequences, than anything else that had
happened or would happen at Camp Hagan until 1970, the end of Hagan
as a girls' camp.

Crashing thunder echoing through the mountains, flashes of lightning,
seeming frighteningly close, sheets of rain in local downpours – Pocono
residents were used to these summer storms. Campers at Hagan came to
enjoy them – safe in the cabins with water pounding on the shutters and
later dripping off lightly, at once exciting and reassuring. There were
always rainy spells, rainy summers, or record-breaking heat waves when
campers took salt pills, the river was low, the land dry, and the campus
brown. These were the normal swings of climate, weather, and river
conditions. Camp life was definitely affected by the state of the river –
too high to swim, too low to canoe, or too full of bottom purge to bear.[42]

Campers and tourists, as well as local residents, were beguiled by the
gentle hills and more or less benign temperatures. There were highs and
lows, of course, but it wasn't Mississippi or Minnesota. A lovely river,
normally docile, with a shallow channel, the Delaware is the longest free-
flowing river in the United States.[43] People felt affection for the river,
and some, including Hagan campers, felt more spiritual attachments, as
had the native Americans before them.

We know that in the first half of the 20th century an important camp
goal was to immerse girls and boys in nature, safely. But safety and

nature don't always go together. Nature cannot be personified, and it certainly cannot be controlled. In the extreme, nature is unpredictable. The hurricanes Connie and Diane and the flooding they caused were, in a sense, the beginning of the end for the river camps, Hagan, Miller, and Ministerium.

By the mid-fifties, the Pocono area had changed significantly from 1937 when Camp Hagan first opened. A lot of undeveloped land had been paved over for parking lots, stores, and large housing developments. Economically, however, the upper Delaware valley remained rural, agricultural, after other areas had benefitted from post WWII economic growth. For farms, the deaths of young men in the war affected the economy perhaps more than in more affluent, suburban or urban areas.

The Poconos saw severe heat in the summer of 1955, setting all-time records of above ninety degrees. Records were also set for lack of rainfall. Local residents were said to fear the worst drought ever in Eastern Pennsylvania. Temperatures had been high since February, and because of calm weather all summer, the water in the Atlantic was heated to a lower depth than normal.

Hurricanes Connie and Diane were a result of what is known in meteorology as a "Bermuda High." Under this condition, a rotating weather system sets up high above Bermuda and the neighboring ocean, a system that pushes hurricanes west and then north. Connie and Diane were caught up in this pattern. The two hurricanes hit the mid-Atlantic coast less than five days apart.

As they made their way up the Atlantic coast, the winds decreased from hurricane to tropical storm rating. However, as the Bermuda High continued to force winds to the northwest, they picked up enormous quantities of water from the deeply warmed waters along the coast. As they moved, they carried that water inland and dumped nearly two feet of rain in the upper Delaware valley in a short time, too short for the overfilled creeks above the source of the Delaware and its tributaries to recover. The Poconos were the hardest hit in Pennsylvania, with Mt.

Pocono receiving twenty inches.[44]

There was no early warning system then. Weather forecasting was relatively primitive in the mid-'50s. Most people did not own a television but got their news from radio, or even slower, from newspapers. There were local weather readings, but they remained local, with no means of compiling weather data over large areas. Connie was the first hurricane to be noted by new weather stations in the Caribbean, but radar units then had only a short range of coverage and transmission. Diane made landfall on Wednesday, August 17th, in North Carolina, then "recurved" up to Pennsylvania and New England.[45] However, after Connie, with the limited information that folks in the Poconos had, and with newspapers announcing that Diane was worn out and expected to lose force, the tourist season continued. Nothing prepared anyone for the smashing power of two hurricanes "in train" and loaded with water hitting the mid-Atlantic coast. Water, not wind, would turn out to be the bigger problem.

Because of the lack of rain earlier in the spring and summer, the ground was dry and hard, and when it had soaked up what it could, which happened very soon, the water went where it would, in low areas, down any channel that led to the next creek or tributary in the Brodhead watershed, leading ultimately to the Delaware. The Brodhead Creek running between Stroudsburg and East Stroudsburg was one such waterway. Some counselors who were in East Stroudsburg for their day off on that Thursday, August 18th volunteered with the Red Cross and worked that evening creekside, near the rising water, helping residents get to safety. Roadways also made good channels for the water. The area included Milford and Dingman's Ferry, familiar to Hagan canoers.

What happened at the river camps? Early Friday morning, August 19th at Camp Miller, the water was coming up over the cabin floors, at one point so high a Miller camper saw the trailer of an eighteen-wheel truck float by. Some counselors paddled canoes through a cabin and the Mess Hall. Eventually the cabins floated off their cinderblocks. The boys were rescued in a human chain of campers and counselors, getting everyone to higher ground. Everyone was safe, but Camp Miller was pretty much wiped out.

Although the waters did not rise above Camp Hagan's river bank, which was higher than Miller's, because of great concern, widespread evacuation, and so much damage in the area, Hagan closed early and all campers and most staff were sent home. Ruth Clegg Whitsel saw a house float by. She says, "It went by so fast, I couldn't believe what I was seeing!" Girls packed up their things. Some campers were taken to Camp Mini, others into Stroudsburg, while some waited for parents to arrive to retrieve them or to be picked up by buses. On Saturday, August 20th a small piece in the *Easton Express* informed parents that on Sunday their children would be delivered "at the cloverleaf intersection of Routes 611 and 402 near Stroudsburg, where they can be picked up during daylight hours." *The Philadelphia Inquirer* later reported 10,000 children evacuated from Pocono summer camps. Many got off chartered Greyhound buses at Reading Terminal in Philadelphia. Hagan and Miller campers were apparently the third group to arrive, others having come in the night before. Most of Hagan and Miller campers were actually taken to Allentown. According to the *Inquirer*, there were lots of tears. Fear? Relief? No, sadness at leaving camp!

The girls couldn't know then the extent of the disaster that had occurred. There was even greater destruction in New England from Connie and Diane, but deaths in the Delaware Valley and watershed alone were nearly 100. Some irrecoverable old hotels, residences, and shopping areas in towns, as well as old covered bridges, farms, and country stores along the creeks which were tributaries to the Delaware and had overflowed their banks, were replaced with large chain stores and other commercial and residential development. Many farms and old homesteads were never rebuilt, indeed couldn't have been rebuilt, as the materials of that life had washed away.

Camp Miller was cleaned up, rebuilt, and open the next summer. Mary Shafer in *Devastation on the Delaware* suggests the new Camp Miller was somewhat less rustic, not surprising since the original was built in the 1920s. According to the *Minutes,* with volunteer work by the

143

Lutheran Brotherhood and donations from churches, "all camps were in splendid physical condition for the 1956 season."

It is in this sense that Connie and Diane were the beginning of the end for Camp Hagan. Camp Miller was rebuilt and at Hagan there was not significant damage. But a way of life in the Poconos, emerging after WWII, moved abruptly along a path of change. And then, various authorities perked up their ears and started talking once again about dams on the Delaware and the larger tributaries for flood control. This was a longstanding conversation, and its renewal would have powerful effects in the years to come. The issue of dams was back on the table.

Endnotes

---

[42] Postel and Richter, *Rivers for Life*.

[43] Source, unless otherwise noted, is Shafer's *Devastation on the Delaware*.

[44] Shafer, p. 13

[45] Shafer, p. 467

Chapter 11
The Beginning of the End
The Tocks Island Dam Project

*I first heard of the Tocks Island dam project in 1961 when I was 11 and
just about to go off to my third summer at Hagan. I was devastated at
that young age that Hagan might not be around forever. I'm so lucky
that I was able to spend twelve summers at Hagan.*
Molly Le Van

Even before Camp Hagan was established, a U.S. government power
project had already been proposed, to build several dams on the
Delaware and use the Delaware River Valley as a watershed. In 1936 the
Synod was worried about going forward with any more development at
Camp Miller while this was a possibility. Nevertheless, plans for Hagan
were begun.

The idea of building a dam on the Delaware lay dormant for years,
until the drenching passage of hurricanes Connie and Diane over
Northeastern Pennsylvania with the resultant flooding, damage, and loss
of lives.

In 1960, the Synod *Minutes* record the first mention since 1939 of the
plans by interstate and federal governments for damming the Delaware.
The dam would be at Tocks Island, north of the Delaware River Water
Gap, well south of Dingman's Ferry, and would "engulf all 3 camps and
necessitate new camp sites."[46] The Army Corps of Engineers reported
as early as 1956 that a dam at Tocks Island would not have helped against
the flooding from the hurricanes, but this finding was not widely known.
And that was not even the first such study. In 1942 and 1945 local or
state governments had rejected such a project because of geological
problems. But the Federal Flood Control Act of 1962 had no public
hearing. The Lutheran *Minutes* note that the expected completion of
Tocks Island Dam was 1975. A committee was appointed by the Synod

to start looking for camp sites, and purchase agreements were signed in 1963 for 3000 acres in Bear Creek Township, Luzerne County, with the expectation that a lake would be developed there.

The Tocks Island Dam Project was proposed to Congress in 1965. The dam would provide both reservoir and recreation, so businesses and developers were intent on its completion. The reservoir would be thirty-seven miles long, up to Port Jervis,[47] and a mile wide (including Sunfish Pond, known earlier as Hidden Lake) and up to 140 feet deep. Approximately 600 families and property owners, some who had lived and worked the land for generations, would be displaced through condemnation and grudging sales or seizure by eminent domain. According to Shafer in *Devastation on the Delaware,* local protests included road signs which read "A Pox on Tocks."[48]

After Nancy Gotwalt resigned as Director of Camp Hagan for reasons of health before the 1968 season, the Synod camp committee in May was still interviewing applicants for the position. There is a sense of disorganization, disintegration – this has never happened before. A year later, the Synod announced that, by agreement with the dam commission, Hagan would continue through 1969 and 1970. They hoped facilities would soon be available at the new site. According to the *Minutes*, the 1969 season was "not an especially good one" because of poor communication with pastors and congregations: some people thought the camps were full or thought they were closed because of the project. The Camp Hagan population was down about fifty girls.

In 1970 the Corps of Engineers took possession of the three campsites. The *Minutes* note that the government's final offer was far below the replacement value. An architect was chosen for the development of the Bear Creek site, and the Synod would lease back the Hagan site until they could move.

In spring 1970 Deborah Lindenmuth was still recruiting for staff, and that summer would have no full-time camp director. In this last year of Hagan as a girls' camp, the Lutheran *Minutes* note that the "new program is less structured, giving campers freedom to choose from a variety of

147

offerings."

The Tocks Island Dam project loomed over the camps for all of the 1960s. Camp went on, however, and calendar, schedule, activities, and events were, for much of the decade, "normal," full of fun and learning, traditions and friendship.

Endnotes

---

[46] The original spelling was "Tock's" but contemporary usage dropped the apostrophe, so the spelling is now "Tocks."
[47] Shukaitis, p. 372
[48] Shafer, p. 439

Chapter 12
The Last Generation
Q and A with the Hagan Hags

For the times they are a-changin'
Bob Dylan

A few girls from an intermediate cabin are walking behind the cabins, towels and soap boxes in hand, heading for the shower house in back of the junior unit. It's their day to shower. They close the door, turn on the showers – and put their washcloths over the drain. When there's enough water, they slip and slide across the floor, squeals of laughter echoing in the little building. They are unsupervised and probably not safe. But it's great fun.

***

On Hagan Christmas morning, the CITs are on the rooftop of Great Hall, in their pajamas, laughing and waving. This becomes a traditional part of Hagan Christmas. In the '40s and '50s everyone came to breakfast in pajamas, but CITs on the rooftop? Never. In fact, Sis Wenrich, director from 1948 to 1954, when told of this escapade, is reported to have said "Not on my watch, they wouldn't!" A CIT from the '50s says, "It would never have occurred to us to get up on the roof, or to ask permission to do it!"

150

***

Although most of Hagan's practices, attitudes, and policies remained the same or changed very little from the late 1930s to the late '50s, these two stories show that in the '60s the times were indeed changing, including at Camp Hagan, Shawnee-on-Delaware.

The 1950s had been, in many ways, a golden time. The U.S. economy soared after World War II as industry expanded. "A chicken in every pot" for the middle and working classes was pretty much realized, and soon a car in the driveway, too. Despite some growing racial and cultural problems, still unacknowledged by much of the population, people were optimistic for their own future and their children's future. Parents who sent their children to summer camp would generally have been a part of such social and economic groups.

News Flashes *Hagan Herald* 1964
–The Beatles are coming to the U.S.A. in the fall.
–Mayor Wagner and Martin Luther King are talking about the race trouble[s].

Discussing culture by decades can be misleading and inaccurate. In this book, such references are a convenience for talking about Hagan's history, but only that – a convenience. As with most "eras," the '60s have murky boundaries. Some historians mark the beginning of the '60s with Martin Luther King's leading the Montgomery bus boycott and the publication of Allen Ginsberg's *Howl*, both in 1955. On the other hand, the so-called "'60s" may not have begun at an Eastern Pennsylvania church camp until mid-decade, and perhaps not very dramatically then.[49]

Also, it's hard to separate that nationwide social change from the local fears, anxiety, and anger about the Tocks Island Dam project, which meant that soon Camp Hagan, the river camps, and local Minisink life would all go away.

Noticeable differences in behavior, however, were occurring. For example, few counselors had a car on campus in earlier decades, but several did in the '60s, making possible not only conveniences but also transgressions that simply couldn't have occurred earlier. Even more revealing, Director Deborah Lindenmuth, 1968-69, was allegedly (reported by several '60s camper/counselors) appointed to restore order, suggesting that perhaps things were feeling a bit disordered. So, social changes, along with the knowledge that Hagan would soon end, had an effect on Hagan camp life.

Campers and counselors in the '40s and '50s had a good time at Camp Hagan, but the '60s girls had a good time in some different ways. They were a rowdy bunch; not all, of course, but enough to put a stamp on the decade at Hagan, the "laughter stamp." For example, girls who slept in the upper bunks wrote or carved their names and years into the wall, leaving a colorful and happy record of their presence. As '50s camper and longtime resident of upper bunks Pat Ulrich Ritter says, "We wouldn't even have thought of it!"

As we look at Camp Hagan in the '60s, the goal is to understand how Hagan life stayed the same and how it changed. Because much of what remained the same has been told in previous chapters, to avoid redundancy, this section will focus mostly on newness and difference, and still address what girls experienced and how they felt about their experiences.

The directorship was one important source of continuity at Hagan. From 1938 until 1959, every director except the very first had served for at least two years, some (Jane Taylor, Esther Wenrich, Jane Endres Hock) for several more. This pattern continued to contribute greatly to the stability of Hagan life. Sis Wenrich, Jane Endres Hock, Phyllis Wiest Gilbert, Robin Fidler Brancato, and Linda Brandt Barr had all been campers, and most were CITs and JCs, counselors and department heads, too. Although the women in the first half of the '60s were co-directors with their husbands (having a married couple was a new experience for the Lutheran Board – in 1961 they found it "most satisfactory"), the fact that they already knew Hagan history and traditions was a big factor in ensuring stability into that decade.

1960   Phyllis Wiest Gilbert and John Gilbert
1961   Robin Fidler Brancato and John Brancato
1962-65 Linda Brandt Barr and Clyde Barr
1966-67 Nancy A. Gotwalt
1968-69 Deborah Lindenmuth
1970 Executive Director Rev. Roy E. Gulliford

Not so, however, in Hagan's later years. Nancy A. Gotwalt, 1966-67, and Deborah Lindenmuth, 1968-69, who each served two years, were both entirely new to Camp Hagan. They relied on the knowledge of experienced staff or their own experience in other camping organizations. Regardless of personality and approach, this leadership role cannot have been easy. Hagan was by then long established and well set in its ways. Returning campers and counselors, and there were always many, expected things to remain the same. On the other hand, some campers in the '60s were perhaps more ready for change, questioning the damp old CIT tents, the two-seater toilet in the senior shower house, or the homey ritual of taking the beds out of the cabins and scrubbing the floor every Friday morning. (None, so far as we know, ever got tired of washing hair in the river.) Such issues had to be dealt with by women who had no Hagan history to fall back on.

What's new on the campus?

Some new housing for department heads and staff appeared. Next to the Junior Unit, the Barn replaced the former Shack, and the Palace, near the waterfront stairs, held the Waldorf on the second floor and the new porch on the river side, with a big screened-in area for a staff lounge. Also new were the Arts and Crafts building, erected in 1959, and the expanded Pill Box (medical services). Several more volleyball and badminton courts now lined the riverbank on the senior end. Campers had muttered for years about the folly of weeding and rolling tennis courts too hard-packed and bumpy to use, and finally in the mid-'60s the courts morphed into a graveled lot.

The trees, planted some twenty to twenty-five years previously in

153

front of the cabins, were, by the '60s, big and full. The pines encircling the Council Fire and in the Outdoor Chapel towered above everything. Mature trees lined the entrance drive, and the campus that Posie Clymer, one of the earliest campers, had described as "wide open and bare" looked well-used and well-kept.

Unchanged, the three central buildings, Great Hall, the Rat Trap, and the Korn Kribbe, still anchored the camp.

The underbrush on the river bank had recovered from the trauma of the 1955 hurricanes and flood. The general aura remained simple, somewhat plain, comfortable, and welcoming.

And the Campers?

Many campers still came from the Allentown-Bethlehem and Philadelphia areas of Pennsylvania, a few from New Jersey, New York, Connecticut, and very occasionally from other eastern states. In these years, more campers came from fewer locations compared to previous decades. And in our small sample there appear to be more campers from urban areas, as the country itself was continuing urbanization begun earlier in the century.

By this time some campers, like Mary Goldsmith Westhuis, had mothers who had been at Hagan. Judy Meseroll Scalzitti's mother, Lois Jack Meseroll, was at Camp Hagan from 1939-1942 and Judy's uncle, Lois's brother, attended Camp Miller. Dotty Watson Westgate's mother, Betsy Fenstermacher, "some time in the earliest day") also was a Hagan camper. Janet Brooks's mother, Dottie Mueller, was an early camper and had helped to build the stone altar.

In the '50s, camp fees had risen to $32

My mom, Kit Reinbold, was first head of the Hagan Waterfront in 1937 and my dad, Charles Goldsmith (previously a camper and counselor) was camp doctor at Miller. My mom's brother, a counselor at Miller, introduced them. Spending the month of August at Hagan was never a choice. Good thing I loved it there!
Mary "Marygold" Goldsmith Westhuis

154

a week, with a Lutheran discount of $2. In 1966 the fees were $37, still with a $2 discount for Lutherans. However, in 1970, Hagan's last year as a girls' camp, the fees climbed to $55 for non-Lutherans, $45 for Lutherans. The 1970 synod *Minutes* note that funding for Hagan was difficult because the two synods (Northeast and Southeast) "give the lowest per camper subsidy of all the LCA synods." Despite financial limitations, and reflecting broader social concerns, the synod created a "campership" (scholarship) program, which in its first year served ninety-two children from the Northeastern and Southeastern Pennsylvania Synods at Camp Hagan and Camp Miller.

Diversity? Not so much. The proportion of Lutherans to non-Lutherans hovered around 60% to two-thirds. The remainder were seldom other than mainstream Protestant. Sometimes counselors brought Jewish friends from college to be on staff, and there was an African-American nurse one year, as well as a few African-American campers, one Latina, and a black CIT.

> *Race was not a subject for jokes, nor did we hear demeaning statements about anyone whose skin wasn't white.*
> Barb Belon

So, Camp Hagan was made up of middle class girls and young women – a few upper-mid, a few lower-mid, but basically white, Protestant, middle class folks. Camp Hagan and the other two river camps were avowedly for and of Lutherans. Although the freedom marches and school integration were '60s events, it would take some years, even decades, for these principles to become part of education and society. At Hagan, in religion classes, campers discuss prejudice and racial and ethnic issues.

CITs

The experience of being a CIT in the '60s reflected a trend toward the professionalization of careers from business to nursing, with increased amounts of formal training and close supervision. Modeled on preparing teachers, more attention was now paid to preparing CITs. In pre-camp week, CITs had lessons on teaching in the departments and on being

155

cabin counselors. They were regularly mentored and evaluated. Dotty Westgate describes how these changes sometimes created conflicting definitions of CITs:

> According to one CIT head who tried to keep us in check, we were only "privileged campers." Hmmmmm. Privileged campers who got to come a week early and do all the dirty work, poop four inches away from each other in the moldy shower house, write lesson plans, take care of and teach the campers. But we also got to sing the cool song with salt shakers, climb onto the roof on Christmas morning, take days off to buy candles in New Hope or swim in someone's pool, and know that we had been chosen for these honors!

What do you remember about counselors?

Wonderful role models. People that talked to you, listened to you, cared about you, asked questions, guided you. I don't see how it can get any better than that.

Barb Belon

Remember the old wheelbarrows used to tote luggage from the parking lot to the cabins in the first years? Then handcarts and more technologically advanced versions – a truck-pulled dolly and finally the old station wagon – all to save the grass. No driving up to the cabins, ever! The '60s were the CITs' glory years – after marking the cabin destination in chalk on baggage as the families unloaded, they got to ride on the tailgate, from parking lot to cabins and back. In the last couple of years, however, there was a big change in this procedure. As concerns grew regarding Tocks Island Dam and the camp's fate, it was as if someone in the administration said, *Oh, never mind, let 'em drive up to the cabins.*

Cabin Life
Most campers from all Hagan times do not recall any bullying or

negativity. Some '60s camper/counselors simply say no – no cliques or making fun of misfits. Some say a little teasing, not really bullying. One suggests that girls being girls, there would always be someone no one liked and some tight circles of long-time camp friends. Another says once her cabin mates teased her about her long legs but she took it as friendly, not mean.

Here we must step back and remember that our sources are those who stayed at Camp Hagan for many years and mostly loved it. Our sample is a bit skewed toward positive feelings. Maybe those stories are all lost with the campers who never came back. 1960s' campers acknowledge that girls who returned year after year may have seemed like cliques to newcomers, and a few rue having in private made fun of a special-needs camper, but overall the stronger memory is of trying to help girls who might need it. The general ethic was *make friends, be friends.*

Pranks

> *Didn't everyone short sheet their counselor's bed?*
> Barb Dando

If college students and hippies were more rebellious and precocious than earlier generations, what about campers? 1940s and '50s camper/counselors agree that '60s girls were much more inventive about pranks and admire their ingenuity: they made a spider web with string about an inch above a camper's head while she was sleeping, put a mattress in a tree on a Friday scrub morning, and took out a cot with the camper sleeping in it so she'd wake up outside. Another camper found toothpaste on the toilet seat – that's a new one.

Change Days and Visiting Days

What's a funny thing you remember?

157

Skinny dipping one hot evening with comrades and half the camp on top of the steps watching.

Mitzi Mowldes

Levitating tables. On staff in 1968 and '69, there were a few times after taps when we gathered in Great Hall and had the tables rocking! Maybe a couple of legs came off the floor, but I don't remember being successful with all of them.

Barb Belon

Until 1968, Hagan maintained the Change Days and Visiting Days established in the mid-'50s, with campers arriving and leaving on Saturday, every two weeks. But in 1969 the method of registration changed: after the opening two weeks, registration was on Sunday, instead of Saturday as in the past, with special programs on Saturday and Sunday of change weekends for campers.

> *On Fridays after hair wash we were allowed to wear our own tops – supposedly because we couldn't get the uniform top over a head full of rollers, although many of us just wore t-shirts anyway.*
> Susan Davit Maxwell

Through most of the '60s, visiting was limited to Change Day weekends. Now, however, for the first time, parents could take their children out of camp to do laundry or have a meal. Then in the last two years, the camp was cleared entirely of campers on change-day weekends. Every two weeks all campers went home on Saturday and returned on Sunday every two weeks, and the counselors had their own visitors, went on float trips on the river, and basically had the weekend off. Fine for the counselors, but surely a headache for the parents. This arrangement amazes campers from previous times. A little chaotic. The sound of things coming to an end.

A new dress code had been adopted in 1957, consisting of brown shorts and a white middy blouse, worn by all on Sundays and by staff on change-days. Daily uniforms cost $3.85, the dress uniform, $4.50.

Director Nan Gotwalt made the change to Bermuda length shorts in 1966. Recall the '50s campers who "pegged" their shorts, or rolled them up as high as they could and then tucked them under. In both periods, '50s and '60s, campers made the uniforms their own with small adjustments.

> *Nan Gotwalt showed the new Bermuda shorts at a Christmas reunion of staff and commented on how the back seam was extra wide so we could let them out as necessary. I blurted out "Let them out? We always take them in!"*
> Susan Davit Maxwell

The Day

> *I loved scrub day each week.*
> Martha Conboy

Instead of gathering on cabin porches, where campers and counselors discussed issues, in the last few years of Camp Hagan, Morning Watch again became an all-camp gathering in Great Hall before breakfast. This last Morning Watch consisted of a reading only, with no discussion by campers and counselors.

What do you especially remember about flag raising?

I remember standing in the big triangle around the flag pole every morning and the sun beating on us (why did we not wear sunglasses or hats back then?) and nearly fainting every morning
Jane Terry

Kaper Chart

	Sunday	Monday	Tuesday	Wednesday	Thursday	Friday	Saturday	Sunday	Monday	Tuesday	Wednesday	Thursday	Friday	Saturday
WAITRESS	1	2	3	4	5	6	7	8	9	10	11	12	1	2
GREAT HALL	2	3	4	5	6	7	8	9	10	11	12	1	2	3
SHOWER HOUSE	3	4	5	6	7	8	9	10	11	12	1	2	3	4
ARTS AND CRAFTS 4:15	4	5	6	7	8	9	10	11	12	1	2	3	4	5
FLOOR AND Porch	5	6	7	8	9	10	11	12	1	2	3	4	5	6
OUTSIDE BACKLINE BACK SINK	6	7	8	9	10	11	12	1	2	3	4	5	6	7
BASIN, Bucket and John	7	8	9	10	11	12	1	2	3	4	5	6	7	8
Beds and Cubbies	8	9	10	11	12	1	2	3	4	5	6	7	8	9
FLOOR	9	10	11	12	1	2	3	4	5	6	7	8	9	10
CLOSET	10	11	12	1	2	3	4	5	6	7	8	9	10	11
SHUTTERS and Ledges	11	12	1	2	3	4	5	6	7	8	9	10	11	12
PUSSIES COBWEBS BASKET	12	1	2	3	4	5	6	7	8	9	10	11	12	1

Following the latter part of the '50s, when cabin groups began moving as a unit, it was the OD's job to get the schedule from the Rat Trap porch (Martie Davis recalls that the slide-in board was made for Hagan by Camp Miller).

160

Meals and Mealtimes

Knowing the day of the week by the meal

After the CIT production of *Mary Poppins*, all singing "Let's Go Fly a Kite" while waving a white napkin over our heads.

Singing, bad food, extreme fun

The constant singing – how did we ever eat?

Melamine dinnerware, the smell of the sponge bucket, bug juice, waiting until four people were served to eat, running to sit with favorite counselor, singing grace, singing after dinner, and kitchen boys!

The wonderful murals in Great Hall. Each year a new mural was added, depicting a different part of camp life. I enjoyed looking at them and looking forward to the new addition.

Singing "Announcements, announcements, announcements" to the tune of "National Embalming School."

Rest Hour, which used to be nobody's favorite time, was now inexplicably an hour and a half. As a result, there were only two activity periods in the afternoon, relaxing the jam-packed schedule a bit.

Vespers, one camper recalls, was like group meditation while in Cabin Devotions girls learned to listen and respect others' thoughts. By the '60s the record for Taps was a bit scratchy.

What do you especially remember about evenings?

Jupiter [Hartman] reading Black Beauty to us after Taps, then coming around to each camper to talk just a few sentences.
Diane Shubert Cooke

There's the quiet at night, after Devotions, when taps plays, the candles are blown out, and campers reflect upon their day or start taunting Unit Duty.

Sandy Dempsey

Activities in the Departments

63 steps to the waterfront
Connie Wiegman Robinson

In Aquatics, new steps down to the waterfront were built, and a single tag board at the bottom replaced the two-board system. Canoe trips, always a favorite for these river girls, ventured farther afield than earlier, now to Kittatiny and Milford. For Judy Meseroll Scalzitti, canoeing down the river in the stern for the first time made a special memory.

Arts and Crafts

Lanyards, lanyards, and more lanyards
Almost Everyone

Some girls were happy to spend all day every day in the Craft Shop; many girls, who thought of themselves as athletes or swimmers, got to the Craft Shop and found something to enjoy learning to do. Sandy Dempsey remembers "copper things you banged with nails and hammers," and Nancy Hartman recalls "overly shellacked cedar pins." In later years Barb Belon's mother had a lanyard hanging on her door, with a whistle at the end of it. Several alums taught their children to make lanyards. Gay Moceri still has a wooden letter holder with woodburned initials as well as linoleum block prints. When asked what she remembers most, Susan Maxwell says about Arts and Crafts, "Not much. I wasn't into that. I do remember lanyards!"

> Arts and Crafts Projects
> and Materials
>
> *clay and clay slip*
> *wood carving*
> *wood burning*
> *tie dying*
> *leather crafts*
> *tissue paper flowers*
> *popsicle stick crafts*
> *mosaics*
> *plaster crafts*
> *gimp*
>
> Letty Townsend Chadwick,
> Department Head
> 1965-67

Athletics

While athletics had always been central to the camp experience, during the 1960s the department apparently broadened in concept, stated in the 1966 promotional brochure as helping campers to reach all three of the camp goals, to strengthen physically and to develop socially and spiritually. It's easy to see how athletic activities served to physically fortify and socially broaden Hagan campers. But how would it spiritually deepen? "By placing emphasis on sportsmanship, teamwork, and fair play," qualities that would be learned especially in play days. In 1964 the *Hagan Herald* reports a play day held at Camp Hagan with Camp Akiba, continuing a decades-long tradition with this nearby camp.

Two new sports appear: Tumbling occurs during a few years, with, as one camper says, "ratty old mats and basic routines," and speedball, a combination of soccer and handball, not remembered by many.

> *I remember one class in tumbling. They laid old mattresses on the grass and we went through somersaults, front and back. They lined up one or two campers and we were supposed to take a gentle run and dive over them and roll into a somersault. I did fine until it got up to about 4 people. I chickened out in mid-dive and landed full on the people folded over on the mattresses. Needless to say I didn't try it again!*
> Susan Maxwell

Entertainment

How Hags could come up with simple names like Rat Trap, Great Hall, Stables and Barn, and then name a building Korn Kribbe was beyond me. In the '60s we were spelling it Korn Krib even though there was a sign that spelled it otherwise.
Mary Westhuis

Although television, a mostly passive form of entertainment, had already arrived in homes, entertainment at Hagan was still about campers entertaining themselves and each other. Imagine, for instance, your cabin group being given comic strips and acting them out for the rest of the camp, or making skits, using random items handed out in paper bags. The little stage could be seen from the cement floor and the wooden benches, and campers could enjoy shows by CITs, JCs, or counselors – "Staff Follies," *Funny Girl*, or *Winnie the Pooh*. In 1969 the CITs presented *The Music Man*, and each year Camp Miller presented a show or two.

> *I remember being part of a play (all campers could audition) that was put on in the outdoor theater, using juice cans, with a portion cut out, and a candle burning in it, for lighting.*
> Barb Belon

Hagan girls from all eras enjoyed being outside at night. The Counselor Hunt was a favorite activity. In addition to capture-the-flag and scavenger hunts typical in many American summer camps, Hagan

164

in the '60s added Jell-O Hunts. Elder camper/counselors understand Counselor Hunt but are hard put to see how on earth you hunt for Jell-O. Nancy Renninger Albright explains:

> When you made the Jell-O, you used less water so that it was harder. Then it was cut up into cubes and hidden around camp. Each cabin would try to find and carry back as much Jell-O as they could to their counselor. However, they could not use items like a bucket to carry it. Only their arms and hands and clothes. Some campers used their t-shirt to hold it. The counselor would have a garbage bag to collect the Jell-O. The winning weight would win.

(The response of the mothers who did that week's laundry can be imagined.)

Counselor Hunt
Indoors off limits.
Waterfront strictly forbidden.
We [counselors] could hide
pretty much anywhere on
campus.   Trees were popular.
Mary Goldsmith Westhuis

Movie night was an old tradition, sometimes creating new versions of old traumas.

What do you remember about movies?

One in particular was so bloody (cowboys and Indians) that they stopped the movie and had the counselors take the entire Junior unit back to their cabins. I was in either Jr 2 or 4 that year. Must have made an impression because I can still remember it!

Barb Belon

War of the Worlds – *scared to death!*

Judy Hartman Brewer

165

Old Yeller *and being scared out of my wits – I think I was a*
very young camper when it was shown.
Susan Davit Maxwell

Alfred Hitchcock movies were shown frequently. Camper Ann Lentz Partlow says that the day after Hitchcock's *The Birds* was shown, there was a tree filled with starlings and Ann and friends all ran screaming to Great Hall. The following year after they saw *The War of the Worlds*, as they were going back to the cabins, there was a shooting star and they all screamed and ran again.

Some movie titles '60s
camper/counselors remember:

Bambi
Old Yeller
Please Don't Eat the Daisies (Doris
Day)
Rear Window
Rhapsody in Blue (1945)
Tammy
The Man Who Knew Too Much (Doris
Day sings "Que sera")
War of the Worlds
westerns

Nature

In the Nature Department, a museum was now set up, housing a collection of items found on the Nature Trail, which meandered through the woods along the river bank, or on hikes further afield. Museums are, above all, storehouses of knowledge. Contributing to the Nature Museum visibly preserved what campers worked to learn, moving campers' attention to inquiry, cataloging, and preservation.

> Contributions to the Nature Museum:
> arrowheads
> fossils
> bird nests
> snake skins
> mineral specimens
> owl pellets

Pioneering

In Pioneering, Junior campers now went to the Council Fire Circle, made camp, and slept overnight. Longer overnights for older campers included pitching a tent – earlier campers didn't learn this skill since they never took tents but only slept out in the open. In contrast, campers of the '60s no longer needed to learn how to make a bedroll – everybody had sleeping bags. Just the name "Pioneering" suggests the power of that theme in American history, compared to, for instance, "Campcraft."

What do you remember about hikes?

Yellow soap! [put on skin to guard against poison ivy]
A camper at 2014 Reunion

Religion

After the end of World War II, the Lutheran synod could focus more on its underlying mission of Christian education, beginning in 1946 with the establishment of the Ministerium Camp – a leadership camp, or "a school-camp." In 1948 the convention was starting to consider "the attitude of secularization" and "of questioning belief" that had a hold on students. In 1952 the Lutheran Campus Pastor, Robert H. Gearhart, Jr., noted a decrease in public expression of religious faith. In the mid-'60s a seminarian was appointed to supervise and coordinate classes and introduce a new curriculum for Christian education at all three camps. The Synod in 1966 enacted yet more adjustments "to enrich the Christian education aspects" of the programs.

What do you remember about religion classes?

I [have] a mental picture of a couple of cabins, attending the same scheduled religion class, sitting under one of the maple trees around the Korn Krib, discussing the parables, then trying to write one of our own, in "modern day terms."
Barb Belon

The orientation toward religious education and expression culminates in the White Tie requirement from 1967 to 1970, in which girls were asked to "Discuss the Apostle's Creed and its significance." Nothing so directly drawn from church liturgy had ever appeared before in Hagan requirements. The reference to St. Paul in the Citizenship Award is also new.

1971 Citizenship Award
You have been selected to receive the Citizenship Award of Camp Hagan...You display distinct traits of character that St. Paul has described in his first letter to Timothy. They are righteousness, godliness, faith, love, endurance, patience, and gentleness which together make you a girl living in truth, beauty, and hope...May you allow your faith in Christ Jesus to lead your life so that it will forever reflect these qualities.

Although campers probably wouldn't have noticed, a major change occurred in the Lutheran Synod's yearly sales brochure as well. Where before departments were listed mainly according to size, with Religious Activity always, *always* last, in 1966 the "Religion Department" now appeared first. Many years earlier, in 1936, while Camp Hagan was being planned, the Lutheran *Minutes* show that Camps Director LeRoi Snyder said he hoped for the camps to be less oriented toward recreation and more toward Christian Education. Thirty years later his wish was realized.[50]

All Singing, All the Time

Was Hagan still a singing camp?

Of course! You mean at somepoint there was no singing???
Kris Weckerley Sechler

Most songs were longtime favorites, but the campers in the '60s were the first to grow up with rock 'n' roll. There were other signs of newness. *National Embalming School,* popular for many years, was modernized when the CITs passed a salt shaker around like a microphone. Other campers were enthralled by this creative bit of play-acting. A new grace appeared with the "Johnny Appleseed" song, taken from a 1948 Disney film. And the 1964 Hagan songbook had more than twice as many songs *about* Hagan, what Dotty Watson Westgate calls "rah rah Hagan" songs,[51] than the 1954 version.

> *I have a very clear memory as a camper of Dottie Watson and others walking around outside Great Hall singing the Beatles song, "I get by with a little help from my friends."*
> Carol Feltman Wheeler

The Civil Rights Movement and Women's Movement encouraged a broader sensitivity to personal identities – a sense of who we are in society and how we identify ourselves. The '60s campers and counselors then, and now as alums, speak of themselves as "Hagan hags." The term was used occasionally in earlier years, but the '60s girls really grabbed it. "Hags" comes from the song "We are the Hagan Hags, we wear our hair in rags." Most campers probably didn't know that "rags" referred to a very old way of curling hair, of literally rolling hair up in strips of cloth

169

and, most recent to the '60s, tying them to get Shirley Temple ringlets.

Sexism and racism are apparent in a few songs, though the underlying meanings were not noticeable to '60s campers. "Mammy, O Mammy, ain't it a shame / That Snowball ain't my name" was in the songbook but not sung, unknown to campers. "The Cannibal King with a big nose ring fell in love with a dusky maid," but most campers thought it was "dusty maid," and in fact that's how it was printed in the 1964 songbook. "A Man Without a Woman" was such fun to sing, especially when Miller came to visit, that no one paid any attention to the last line: "But if there's one thing worse in the universe, / It's a woman without a man." These songs had sound effects that only added to the playfulness – "Boom boom!" and "Woo hoo!" – and it was likely that most girls in the '60s were no more aware of the social import than were girls in the years before them.

Singing, according to Judith Hartman Brewer, took place "absolutely and all the time." When asked their favorite songs, many camper/counselors say something like "Just too many to list!" And the singing didn't stop when campers stopped attending camp. Several say they taught Hagan songs to their children and grandchildren. "Tell Me Why" was a favorite grandmother's lullaby. Grace was sung at reunion dinners, too. According to Gay Moceri, a non-Hagan customer at a restaurant identified the group as Hagan alums because they sang grace.

The Blue Tie

Awards indicate the values and abilities that the administration wished to instill in campers as well as what campers were willing to do to be rewarded. A look at one tie award in the middle years, the 1950s, and the last decade, the 1960s, affords concrete examples of changes in values. Mainly, although campers in 1950 and 1970 got the same Blue Tie, differences are worth noting because they show the directions in which the Camp Hagan ethic was evolving. Award requirements in the six departments were always divided among the three Hagan goals: Socially Broaden, Physically Fortify, and Spiritually Deepen.

Camp Citizenship, the first item of Socially Broaden, was always the same, all ties, all years: "A camper must display a spirit of cooperation and sportsmanship in all activities, whether it be in a cabin group, a unit, or camp program as a whole."

In Athletics, we see a turn toward leadership roles: serving as scorekeeper or timekeeper and officiating.[52]

For the Blue Tie in Arts and Crafts in 1966, "Have a perfect tool and clean shop record" evolved into "Be in charge of cleaning up four times." Here, as in Athletics, requirements leaned toward leadership.

The '60s showed an enlarged view of Entertainment, with more attention to planning and staging and requirements of working on scenery, costumes, or properties and of helping backstage during an evening program.

The main change in Nature requirements was that a camper must contribute to the Nature Museum. Martie Davis, head of Nature, explains:

> Anything brought in for a tie requirement had to be documented in a little note about the Indians, the glaciers and the nature of the fossils at Hagan, which bird, which snake, what mineral and why do we find it at Hagan, which owl and under what tree, what did the owl eat and why, and so forth.

This requirement reoriented campers toward the social accumulation of knowledge.

In Pioneering, on an overnight hike a Blue Tie camper was responsible for the fire, cooking, and cleanup. Again, we find leadership emphasized alongside practical knowledge.

Making a Health poster replaces writing ten or fifteen health rules, supplanting memorizing with leadership in the form of selecting what information should appear on a poster for public display.

As we have seen, Religion after 1965 holds place before all other departments, with a curriculum focused on religious education and profession of faith. From 1967 to 1970 we find additions of attending religious classes and of discussing "What does God mean to me?"

The much loved and highly valued Silver Acorn award disappeared in 1967.

Some Very Special Days

May Day – a Hagan tradition from the very earliest years. As before, the queen and her court were entertained with a skit and, as Diane Cooke recalls, "girls dancing around that pole with different pastel colors in their hands." But for a few years, the queen came down the river in a rowboat or canoe – this was definitely a new thing!

The Hagan-Miller dance continued, one each in July and August, alternating camp locations.

What is a special memory for you about the Hagan-Miller dance?

The older girls always had their hair in rollers made of OJ cans at dinner. The song changed but not the basic experience: truck, singing, Miller mail. Riding in the truck, singing, "Tonight, tonight won't be just any night" [from West Side Story].

Carol Feltman Wheeler

Hagan Christmas was the be-all and end-all of special days. In fact, it lasted most of the last week. While earlier counselors as well as campers hung their stockings up on Christmas Eve, '60s staff hung whole pillowcases. Cabin porches were decorated for Christmas – that hadn't been seen in a long time. The Yule Log, a piece of which was saved each year for next year's Christmas, in the '60s was hidden on campus for campers to find.

Christmas 1960s

What is a special memory for you about Christmas?

I always came last session and during the year would think about what I wanted to make for gifts and cards.
Carol Feltman Wheeler

A much-loved part of Hagan life, Council Fire was held on the Friday night at the end of every two-week session. The camp sang "Kneel Always When You Light a Fire" as torch bearers came from the four

Third Torchbearer
With this torch I light the fire of character. At Hagan, may we always remember to speak the truth, to love honor, and to seek beauty that we may be morally strengthened and spiritually deepened.
Ann Tucker, 1970

173

Native American spiritual directions, east, south, west, and north, carrying torches made of – flaming toilet paper rolls! Often, then, a representative from each cabin tossed in a small bunch of sticks tied together, called faggots, with a wish from the cabin.

Many campers from Hagan's last years do not remember the story of Haga-Ann at all (Ch. 8). Haga-Ann, the totem pole at the entrance to Council Fire, as well as Council Fire itself, were among the last vestiges of the Indian theme from early American camping. Campfire was often a deeply emotional experience, serving to unite the camp in a serious, shared, moving hour.

The songs for campfire were special to that event, most of them handed down through the years. "Linger Awhile" was still a favorite. "Follow the Gleam" was sung sometimes at Campfire. Barb Belon says, "I knew it was about the zeal of spreading Christianity ... [but] of course, I didn't know then how much blood was shed, fighting over land that three religions claimed!" During the 1960s "In the Still of the Night" was added to the old standards, along with "Peace I Ask of Thee, Oh River." Girls learned to harmonize at Hagan and the heart-felt sound rose into the dark quiet night.

Imagine the smell of the pines, the big council fire crackling, blazing away, girls seated around inside the circle of trees, and hear the singing – this remains a stirring memory for Hagan campers. At the end campers sang "Remember." [53] When Campfire was over, campers left the Council Fire Circle to return to their cabins, singing "It's Time to Leave."

Totem Pole 1960

174

After the last council fire, everyone went down to the waterfront to float candles, which now entered the water in clear plastic cups. But though the floatation device differed, the sentiments of wishes for Hagan and hopes to return next year held fast.

> It's time to leave, time to say goodbye.
> It's time to leave from our campfire site.
> Another day together has been a lot of fun,
> It's time to leave until another sun.

* * *

So, among many, many features of Hagan life that held constant across its roughly three and a half decades, three main changes had developed:

➢ First, the turn in the tie award requirements toward leadership and shared knowledge building.

➢ Second, the increased emphasis on evangelical Christian religion as an activity and an object for study during the day in addition to the original practices of Morning Watch, Vespers, and Cabin Devotions.

➢ And third, preparations for the construction of the Tocks Island Dam on the Delaware and repercussions for Camp Hagan.

What did campers learn? What did Camp Hagan mean?

Oh, this camp of ours. How it has a hold on us.
Sandy Dempsey

As was true of the decline of men's colleges and women's colleges, the merger of Camp Hagan with Camp Miller had its pluses and minuses, its supporters and detractors, followed by a generation that never knew anything other than a combined camp. Many camper/counselors were uncomfortable at the idea of Hagan becoming co-ed, a change made necessary by the closure of Miller and plans to move everything to Bear Creek in a few years. Some campers who became counselors and DPs (department heads), knowing that Hagan was to become a co-ed camp, stopped going to Hagan at the end of the decade – their camp was a girls' camp. Carol Feltman Wheeler says, "[I learned that] girls can do anything without boys. What a gift my parents gave me, sending me to a girls' camp!"

And after camp, then what? When asked about their main work in life, only a few '60s campers answer "mother" either solely or even along with other jobs. In contrast, women who were mothers in earlier times speak first of mothering and homemaking as their work, then teaching, counseling, and business, these occupations often later in life. Although most '60s alums had families and children when they became adults, they do not mention it as their work. They have families and they have careers and professions. This is very different from the '40s and '50s alums who were mothers in the late '40s, '50s and '60s. The difference in attitude about women's work is significant and visible, affirming our sense of social change growing out of the 1960s.

* * *

What did you learn at Hagan? What was a special accomplishment?

I went on an overnight canoe trip when I was a camper in Intermediate 7. I think I was the youngest person to ever do that.
                                  Nancy Hartman

Canoeing in stern for first time
                                  Judy Meseroll Scalzitti

How to swim, how to make a lanyard, how to get along with many different people, how to smoke.
                                  Susan Davit Maxwell

Lifesaving in the Delaware (much more difficult than in a pool). Getting
                                  176

back into a canoe without tipping (I wouldn't even attempt that now!)
Diane Shubert Cooke

Lifelong friendships.
Pretty much everybody

Hagan did not just fill campers' lives in the summers, or during their adolescence and young adulthood.

What effect did Camp Hagan have on your later life?

When I started teaching (in 1972) and one student called another a faggot I said "Do you realize you just called him a bundle of sticks?
Diane Shubert Cooke

I credit my independence, my good decision-making skills, my ability to work cooperatively, and my sense of fairness to Hagan.
Nancy Hartman

I am who I am (independent, outgoing) as a result of my years at camp.
Judy Mezeroll Scalzitti

I have always considered Hagan to be most important in my character building and creativity. It is what made me a leader in many areas... [I learned] how to get along with all types of people. What I have done in life is credited to Camp Hagan."
Director Lyn Brandt Barr

Why did '60s campers return to Hagan for so many years, as so many before them had? Sandy Dempsey speaks for those whose troubled home lives made Hagan a refuge: "It gave me a respite from a home-life that was traumatic. It was a place that was safe." She was by no means alone in this experience. For Connie Wiegman Robinson, the Hagan summer

177

meant "time away from the pressures of family and school." Hagan offered a healthful, nurturing alternative to difficult situations or to just knocking about the neighborhood.

What opportunity did Hagan give you?

The chance to live outside.
Carol Feltman Wheeler

A time to build friendships and have fun with folks from a wide variety of backgrounds and experiences that I might not have encountered otherwise at those ages.
Judy Hartman Brewer

Away from home, being who I wanted to be.
Mitzi Mowlds Carafides

In retrospect, what did Hagan mean to '60s alums? For Barb Belon the short answer is "Everything." She continues: "Acceptance. True friends. My special place. Tradition. Schedule and organization and shared responsibilities." Susan Davit Maxwell adds, "A place to be happy."

Director Tay said at the end of the 1939 season, "We've reached the end of a perfect summer with thankful hearts for all the joys these days have brought." Echoing Tay many years later, '60s camper Carol Feltman Wheeler speaks for campers and counselors from 1937 to 1970:

What did Camp Hagan mean to you?

JOY.

Endnotes

---

[49] Theodore Roszak coined the term "counterculture" in 1969, with his book *The Making of a Counter Culture*.

[50] The Lutheran *Minutes* of 1936 and 1937 note that Camp Miller was first known as a recreational camp.

[51] *Hagan Newsletter* Sept. 2015.

[52] No change in **Aquatics** as the camp continues to adhere strictly to Red Cross guidelines.

[53] *Remember* was sung at YM-YWCA camps.

Chapter 13

The End

When the idea of the Tocks Island Dam resurfaced in 1960, the Synod camp committee expected several more years at the present sites, which they did get. Camp Hagan stopped being a girls' camp in 1971 when the Miller property was given up and Miller boys joined Hagan girls for several years of co-ed camp. The camp committee reported to the Synod that "the merger of Miller and Hagan was accomplished with much less difficulty than had been anticipated" and "few would want to go back to pre-coed days." Camper/counselors who had been at Hagan for many years were not entirely thrilled, while those who had begun at Hagan in the last years of the '60s adapted to the new scene well.

Miller-Hagan

I went into it kicking and screaming. But it turned out to be a fantastic camp, thanks to the many wonderful staff who bent over backwards to help us all get along.
Sarah Buck

Before the merger with Camp Miller, after that property was sold, and before the final move to Bear Creek, where a whole new camp ambiance, program, and purpose would be constructed, life for Haganites changed in ways large and small.

No more uniforms, no May Day, and while Hagan sang in Great Hall after meals, it is said that some Miller counselors preferred to sit out on the steps and smoke.

And Carol Wheeler says, "The last two years of camp, we actually cleared the camp of kids on change weekends: campers had to go home and staff had the weekend off! We did staff float trips and hikes, and had our own visitors. It was really fun for us, but I don't imagine the parents liked it."

To alums from earlier years, this picture is amazing.

In 1972, Congress declared Sunfish Pond (what earlier campers knew as Hidden Lake) a National Landmark, so it could not be used to hold a "pumped-storage power project."[54] This was, legally, the beginning of the end. The enthusiastic plans of federal and commercial interests for the project played out in ways that geologists could have predicted, and indeed did predict, although such warnings seemed to carry no weight when early decisions were being made.

In 1974, at a summit meeting of the governors of the four adjacent states, the dam project was finally killed by massive environmental opposition and a lack of funding due to the great costs of the Vietnam War.[55] In 1978 the final blow was struck when the mid-Delaware was included in the National Wild and Scenic Rivers Act – no structural projects would be allowed.

Even before the Hagan-Miller merger, the Synod was starting to use the Bear Creek site for senior high campers from Camp Mini in 1968, where they would experience "the challenge of surviving in a rugged setting." This goal takes us back to very early camping ideals, an echo of the late 19th and early 20th centuries (Ch. 1). The river camps moved to Bear Creek, near Wilkes-Barre, in 1977 as part of Lutheran outdoor ministries. For a while, homeless people lived in the Camp Hagan cabins. Many long-time farmers and home owners had had to give up their properties, and ultimately pretty much everything was razed to make way for the water that would cover the land once the Tocks Island Dam was built.

It wasn't until 1992 that Congress removed the Tocks Island Dam Project from the list of pending constructions.

Thus unfolds our story, from the forward movement and retreat of the great glacier, leaving the land on which Minsi Lenape tribes lived and hunted, upon which the settlers carved out a new existence, and where Hagan girls and women made their home in summer months, unsuitable for construction of the size and weight of the proposed dam. All that glacial rubble – sand, silt, pebbles, rocks, boulders – was unstable for anything more than a tipi or a house and a bridge.

European settlement displaced the Minsi Native Americans, who had lived in the area since about 8000 BCE. They ranged freely over the land, aside from tribal tiffs over hunting rights. Nobody "owned" the land. It was there, like air and water and animals, and humans were grateful participants. In contrast, European settlers owned their land and residences, and the Lutheran Synod owned the land where the three river camps were established. The change in views of relationship to the land in a sense was the undoing of both the settlers and the campers, because what was owned could be lost, taken away. Ownership turned out not to be a protection.

Ironically, the clearance of the land in preparation for the Tocks Island Dam Project, what Nancy Shukaitis calls the "second exodus" of the Minisink Valley, made it largely the same as when Minsi Lenape Indians lived there.[56] Empty not only of houses but factories, smokestacks, chemical plants, and consumption of natural resources, it was now right for inclusion in the federal parks system, to be known as the Delaware Water Gap National Recreation Area.

* * *

Now, more than half a century later, the area that was Camp Hagan is overgrown, with few distinguishing markers other than trees in special configurations – the double line of trees from the entrance to camp up toward the Rat Trap, the circle of huge pines around the council fire circle, and those that lined the outdoor chapel. Of structures, only the shuffleboard court and Vespers altar remain. Hagan lives for a while longer in the memories of its campers and counselors, and in some of their children and grandchildren, with lanyards, "Tell Me Why," swimming and canoeing, and stories of friends and adventures.

Altar, 1991

Endnotes

[55] Shafer, p. 39
[56] Shukaitis, p. 365

Epilogue

The More We Get Together

Other people may not get it – but
everyone at the reunion does.
Carol Feltman Wheeler

At Hagan reunions, we *re-unite* with those who remember shared experiences and reaffirm our commitment to friendship and love of nature. We find pleasure in catching up, learning about our old friends' lives since we were last together, in some cases not since camp itself. We heal a little bit more the left-over sense of loss, wounds of separation from girls and women whom we lived, played, and worked with and deeply cared for. And we have the chance to swap stories with those who were at Hagan in different years. One of the biggest changes early and middle campers find is that the last generation of campers went together by cabin to activities all through the day, whereas earlier campers had gone individually to any department they chose. Many alums say Hagan reunions cannot be compared to high school or college reunions. We think this is due especially to the atmosphere of safety that pervaded camp life: you can do this, and you'll be all right.

Some reunions were small, informal get-togethers, generally of people living in the same area, such as CITS gathered for a lunch or cabinmates for an overnight at somebody's house. In 2010 Bep Berger wrote gleefully: "Did you know that we had a Camp Hagan Reunion in 1940? It was held at the Rittenhouse Hotel in Philadelphia." She didn't say who was there, but Hagan had only been operating for three or four years – Bep was a camper and her sister, Kit, head of Arts and Crafts. Robin Fiddler Brancato and Inge Woermann Coleman recall gatherings of Hagan CIT and counselor friends as early as 1952, and there were other similar gatherings over the years, in Woodhaven NY, Shawnee and

186

Stroudsburg in the Poconos, Reading, and Philadelphia.

> *At the 2009 reunion I heard a voice beside me saying, So, have you had a good life? I turned and there was Rosie Hallman, whom I hadn't seen since camp decades ago, the audacious question lighting up those mischievous eyes I remembered so well.*
> Alice

Other Hagan reunions of early camper/counselors were larger and more structured, with programs and mailing lists. The first recorded such gathering took place in 1985 at Moselem Springs Restaurant, with a mailing list of forty-one, and another there in 1990. Others took place in 1994 and 1999. Sis Wenrich's 90th birthday was celebrated in 2006 in Blue Bell, PA. Sis, along with Associate Director Kit Berger, anchored the middle years at Hagan. In 2009 a few more alums from the middle years were brought into the fold. Mailing lists were maintained by Kit Berger, Zeke (Liz) Ziegler Hand, and Chris Hill Killough.

And then, after a reunion at Carolyn McGonigle Holleran's in Sinking Spring, PA, in 2009, something wonderful happened. The elder campers discovered the online existence of the '60s alums. Pat Ulrich Ritter (1946-56) wrote to Dotty Watson Westgate (1961-1973) of this find, and Dotty forwarded Pat's message to some of her Hagan friends with the news: *Waddya think of THIS?!!!*

Turns out the '60s camper/counselors had been having their own small informal gatherings and larger organized events well before the two groups found each other. A tri-camp (Hagan, Miller, and Ministerium) reunion was held in Stroudsburg in 2010, with a Hagan Christmas banquet the night before, attended for the first time by camper/counselors from all eras. Another tri-camp reunion in 2012 was reported in the *Pocono Record*, June 23: "Happy campers return decades later to Shawnee." In 2014 a reunion of the three camps was held at Shawnee, with a candle float in memory of deceased Hagan alums. More reunions have followed, with gatherings of Haganites and alums of Camps Miller, Hagan, and Ministerium currently taking place in alternate years. At the time of this writing, a Hagan reunion is to be held at Shawnee in honor of Hagan's 80th birthday (and, coincidentally, that of some attendees.)

Mailing lists have been maintained by Gay Stoudenmaier Moceri, Barb Huffman de Belon, and Sandy Dempsey. Elder campers have gratefully turned over reunion planning and mailing list tasks to '60s women, and camper/counselors of all eras who live far away appreciate the work that those who live closer do to make gatherings possible.

Many alums have said something like, "I was my best self at Hagan" or "I could be who I wanted to be." Now at reunions women in their sixties and beyond get to be the self they have become alongside the campers/counselors with whom they did that early growing. Camper/counselors see each other through the lens of who they once were and learn about the people they have become. Perhaps the bond is even stronger because the camp itself isn't there any more, just the shared tears, laughter, complaints, and achievements.

No longer just gatherings of childhood comrades reaching back to the past to recover connections, reunions occasion a rebirth of friendships, a new phase of our collective lives, a continuing community of Hagan friends.

The more we get together, the happier we'll be.

2009 Reunion of Alums, Early and Mid Years
1st row: guest, Inge Woermann Rau Coleman, Alice Royer Roy,
    Anita Zimmerly Chaney, Martha McGonigle Mewhort,
    Carolyn McGonigle Holleran
2nd row: Peg Detwiler Geers, Robin Fidler Brancato (Dir. 1960),
    Nora Ehrig Kales, Ruth Clegg Whitsel, Elaine
    Emmenheiser Clay, Ginny Steele Grubb, Sis Wenrich,
    Marcia Bard Jefferies, Pat Fletcher, Jane Endres Hock;
Middle row: Betty Stefani MacAdam, Jane Detwiler LeVan, Phyllis
    Wiest Gilbert;
3rd row: Hannelore Freydberg Blew, Chris Hill Killough, Phyl
    Kaspareit Davidson, Rosie Hallman Steen, Lois Eisenhard,
    Patty Pirrault Anderson, Dottie Dutcher Logan, Zeke
    (Elizabeth) Ziegler Hand, Midge Wilkinson Vansant, Pat
    Ulrich Ritter, Bep (Betty) Berger, Janeth Mueller.

Appendix 1: Camp Hagan Directors

1937	Gladys Marie Staub
1938-1945	Jane M. Taylor
1946-1947	Betty Gross
1948	Esther Wenrich Kline
1949 -1952	Esther Wenrich
1953-1954	Edith M. Klain
1955-1957	Jane Endres
1958-1959	Frances Bowden
1960	Phyllis Wiest Gilbert and Edward Gilbert
1961	Robin Fidler Brancato and John Brancato
1962-1965	Linda Brandt Barr and Clyde Barr
1966-1967	Nancy A. Gotwalt
1968-1969	Deborah Lindenmuth
1970	Exec. Dir. Rev. Roy E. Gulliford

Appendix 2: Camp Hagan Staff 1937

Name	From
Gladys Marie Staub	Scranton
Position: Directress	
Catherine E. Walters	Hazleton
Position: Nurse	
Ethel Heidenreich	Reading
Position: Dietician	
Kathryn E. Reinbold (Skipper)	Lansdowne
Position: Directress of Waterfront; Head Counsellor Jr. Camp	
V. Elizabeth Cameron (Zipper)	Allentown
Position: Directress of Pioneer Camping; Head Counsellor Sr. Camp	
Jane C. Randall	Royersford
Position: Waterfront; Head Counsellor Intermediate Camp	
Dorothy L. Bechtel	Reading
Position: Camp Secretary, Business Manager	
Anne K. Minnich (Sunny)	Reading
Position: Directress Arts and Crafts	
Jane Taylor	Allentown
Position: Directress Religious Activities	
Alice G. Finley (A.G.)	Chestnut Hill
Position: Directress Nature Study	
Esther M. Wenrich (Sis)	West Reading
Position: Directress of Athletics	
Naomi Hittinger	Bethlehem
Position: Entertainment, Librarian	
Ruth E. Kistler	E. Stroudsburg
Position: Music	

Name	From
Annabel Brubaker	Lebanon
Position: Athletics	
M. Edwina Croll	
Position: Athletics	
Katherine L. Reumann	Philadelphia
Position: Waterfront	
Jean K. Williams	Palmerton
Position: Waterfront	
Ruth McLaughlin	Philadelphia
Position: Waterfront	
Elinor M. Petersen	Philadelphia
Position: Arts and Crafts	
Lucille S. Maberry	Schuylkill Haven
Position: Athletics	
Herman W. Stoldt (Bear Heart)	Springfield, MA
Position: Associate Director Arts and Crafts	
Mrs. Fred A. Koehler	Bethlehem
Position: Cook	
Jeanne B. Fry	Royersford
Position: Kitchen Help	
Helen Schweitzer	Scranton
Position: Kitchen Help	
Anna I. Steppacher	Philadelphia
Position: Kitchen Help	
Howard Schoellkopf	Camp Miller Farm
Position: Caretaker	

Appendix 3: Charter Campers

First List

Irene Foedisch
Gayle Van Cleve
Barbara Peters
Patsy Callahan
Kathryn Rapp
Ann Stillwagen
Doris Greenleaf
Georgia Callahan
Frances Dodd
Ardath Houser
Dorothy Christman
Betty Jane Scheurer
Susanne Beerli ?
Barbara Bosch
Virginia Johnston
Martha L. Arbogast
Jeanne Chesterman
Catherine Henninger
Doris Burnett
Olive Patchin Weaver
Marjorie S. Brown
Cynthia Lawfer
Nancy H. Vaughan
Mary Jane Anderson
Marilyn Cooper
Rose Marie Hermann
Elizabeth K. Jones
Betsy Fenstermacher

Mare E. Crockett
Jane Carter Horner
Henrietta Hemminger
Ann Small
Eleanor H. Dutton
Ruth Clearwater
Mary Elizabeth Porter
Dorothy Madge Plieskatt
Edith Hermann
Margaret R. Suppes
Marguerite Nearing
Beulah Arbogast
Eleanor McIlvaine
Faith F. (L?)Maxson
Betty Walker
Dorothy Ross
Mary Louise Landis (Landes?)
(Lanc)
Mary Edwards

Second List

Jane Cline
Elizabeth Whetstone
Ruth Burnett
Donna Stewart
Nancy Jane Reed
Jane Detwiler
Patsy Blasius
Henrietta Miller

Rhoda M. Bachman
Margaret McQuillan
Lucille Wehman
Lucille J. Trautvetter
Dorothy R. McCandless
Ruth F. Foedisch
Margaret Graber
Helen Drpon ?
Mary Lou Landis
Jane Schlosser
Sarah Jane Miller
Frances Steeley
Miriam Blasius
Marie A. Richards
Jeannette Arbogast
Henrietta S. Nixon
Dorothy J. Nixon
Sara Elyn Stump
Betty Campbell
Geraldine H?
Ernestine Hasskarl
Dorothea Hasskarl
Martha E. Coffin
Emilie Frantz
Frances J. Piesce ?
Josephine Pittinger
Henrietta Brink
Evelyn Ann Wilson

Appendix 4: Questionnaires

Questionnaire 1

Your name:
Address:
Phone number:
Email:

1. What is your date of birth?
2. Where did you grow up?
3. Did you go to college or other school after high school?
    Where/what?
4. What was your major or field of study?
5. What degree(s)/certificates did you get?
6. In your life, what was your main work/job?
7. Were you a camper at Camp Hagan? YES NO
8. What years?
9. How did you come to go to Camp Hagan?
10. Who was/were the director(s) when you were a camper?
11. Do you remember the Assistant Director(s)?
12. What cabins were you in as a camper? Please tell us the counselors,
    if you recall them:
13. Can you remember other campers who came up with you? If
    possible, can you give cabins and years?
14. Were you a CIT? If yes, when?
15. Who was head of CIT's/JC's then?
16. Were you a JC? If yes, when?
17. Who was head of CIT's/JC's then?
18. Were you a counselor? What years?
19. What cabin(s) did you have?
20. Who was the unit head?

21. Who was/were the director(s) when you were a counselor?
22. Do you recall the Assistant Director(s)?
23. As a counselor, what department(s) were you in?
24. Were you a department or unit head? YES NO
25. If YES, What department(s) / unit?
26. What year(s)?
27. Who was/were the nurse(s) when you were at Hagan?

Thank you so much for giving your time and energy to responding.
    You are much appreciated! Alice Royer Roy

Questionnaire 2

Your name:

1. If you were at the 2009 reunion at Carolyn McGonigle Holleran's:
    Carolyn asked us each to say a brief memory of something about
    camp, mostly short phrases, like "Canoe trips" or "camp fires."
    What did you say?
2. Please tell a little more about that. What were you thinking about,
    any specific event or description?
3. If you weren't at the reunion, please imagine that you are sitting in a
    big circle with Hagan friends. What would you say in answer to
    Carolyn's question?
4. When were visiting days when you were at Hagan?
5. When were change days?
6. Do you remember special event days? Please tell as many as you
    can:
7. What evening entertainments do you recall?
8. Did you see movies at camp when you were a camper (or
    counselor)?
9. If yes, can you remember some titles?
10. And if yes, where were the movies shown?

11. What are some rules and regulations you remember?
12. What do you recall about campfire? Stories? Songs? Pageants, skits? Haga-Ann?
13. When were campfires held in your years at CH? (Every week? every two weeks?)
14. What did you make in Arts and Crafts?
15. What is your favorite camp song?
16. What's a special memory for you at Hagan?
17. What's the funniest thing you remember happening at Hagan?
18. What things were new for you at camp? (sights, smells, sounds, tastes, experiences?)
19. What did camp mean to you?
20. What were your fears, going to camp for the first time?
21. Did any of your relatives, before or after you, go to Camp Hagan?
22. Did girls trade jobs from the Kaper Chart?
23. Anything special you remember about meals and mealtimes?
24. What was your greatest accomplishment at camp?
25. Do you recall any instances of bullying? Of shutting out unpopular girls? Cliques?
26. Did you ever get into trouble, do something wrong, get scolded? A disappointment? A bad experience? If you're comfortable, please tell the story:
27. Did you ever play a prank on anyone?
28. Why did you keep coming back to camp?
29. When you stopped, why did you stop?

Appendix 5: Biographical Information:

Name	Where Grew up	College or other
Lucille Dissinger Altenderfer	Wyomissing, PA	Albright College
		Institute of Fine Arts
		McCann School of Business
Patricia Pirrault Anderson	Wyndmoor, PA	Pennsylvania State University
Linda Brandt Barr		
Carol Phillips Bauer	Woodhaven, NY	Wilson College York University
Betty M. Berger Berger	Westlawn, PA	Albright College
Hannelore Laurie Freydberg Blew	Forest Hills, NY	Wellesley College
Robin Fidler Brancato	Wyomissing, PA	University of Pennsylvania The City University of New York
Eleanor "Norie" McIlvaine Clague	Jenkintown, PA Fort Washington	University of Pennsylvania College for Women
Posie Bosek Clymer	Cheltenham, PA	Moravian College for Women
Pat Wagenhall Coffey	Summit, NJ	Denison

Campers of 1937-1960

Major	Degree	Main Work
		Tax Preparation
Home Economics	Certif. typing, shorthand	
Elementary Education	BS	Housewife, Taught 3rd Grade
Economics, History, Mathematics	BA, PhD	Directed Camps Including Camp Hagan, Taught School, Held Music Festivals, Have A Tour Company
		Professor of History
Home Economics	BS	Taught Home Economics
Zoology/Physiology	BA	Associate in Ministry, Evangelical Lutheran Church in America: Director of Christian Education and Parish Administrator
Creative Writing	BA MA	Director of Camp Hagan, Teacher, Author of Young Adult fiction and nonfiction
Elementary Education	BS in Education	Homemaker
Medical Technology	BS	Research Laboratory, On A Team That First Measured Cholesterol in A Blood Sample
Art	BA	Computer Programmer/ Analyst/Network Specialist

Name	Where Grew up	College or other
Inge Woermann Rau Coleman	Woodhaven, NY	Mount Holyoke College
		Lab. Institute of Merchandising
		Realtor's Institute (Lansdale)
Phyllis Kaspareit Davidson	Woodhaven, NY	Wilson College
		Chatham College
		Carnegie Mellon
Arlene Piret Dunphey	Westfield, NJ	Centenary College
Sara Jane (Sally) Holstrum Evans	Philadelphia, PA	Pennsylvania State University
Ginny Hausmann Fitzgerald	Drexel Hill, PA	Gettysburg College
	Cranford, NJ	Bentley College
Patricia Fletcher	West Reading, PA	New York University
Carol Jones Fuller	Long Island and Baldwin, NY	Tobé Coburn School of Fashion Merchandise
Peg Detwiler Geers	Norristown, PA	Museum School of Art
Irmgard "Trudy" Hagedorn Geithner	Philadelphia, PA	Moore College of Art & Design

Major	Degree	Main Work
Economics	BA	Relocation Director for Real Estate Company
Marketing	Real Estate Associate License, Broker's License	
Real Estate	Federal funded license for special program in Speech and Language	
American Civilization	BA	Software Engineer, Paraprofessional in Schools, Bookkeeper
Information Science		
Information Systems	MPM Master of Public Management	
Liberal Arts/Business	No Degree	Secretary to Attorney, Administrative Assistant to P President
Elementary Education	BS in Education	Substitute Teacher, Secretary
Psychology	BA	HR Management
Human Resources Management	Certificate in HR Management	
General Studies	Associate degree	TWA Various Jobs
Fashion Merchandizing	2 Year Degree	Raised 4 Children, And Had 3 Bowl Mill Stores
Illustration	Certif. /4 years	Advertising, Rug Design
Textile Design	Diploma	Homemaker

Name	Where Grew up	College or other
Phyllis Wiest Gilbert	Reading, PA	Wilson College
Virginia Lehr Gold	Nazareth, PA	Bucknell University
Virginia Young Steele Grubb	Philadelphia, PA	University of Pennsylvania
Liz (Zeke) Ziegler Hand	Nazareth, PA	Smith College
Pat Sloan Haven	Pennsylvania, Michigan, Ohio	Wilson College Fuller Seminary
Carolyn McGonigle Holleran	Wyomissing, PA	Connecticut College
		Yale University
Marcia Bard Jefferis	Reading, PA	Harcum College
Christine Hill Killough	Wyndmoor, PA	Bucknell University
Betsy Brudereck Lashbrook	Shillington, PA	Wilson College
		Drexel Inst. of Technology
Jane Detwiler Le Van	Reading, PA	Syracuse University
Grace Irene "GI" Trimmer Lefever	York, PA	Kutztown State Teachers College
Betty Stefany MacAdam	Whitehall Twp, PA	East Stroudsburg State Teachers College
		Temple University

Major	Degree	Main Work
Chemistry	BS	School Teacher, Director of Camp Hagan
Education	BS Ed	Teacher
Chemistry/Education	BA, MA	High School Chemistry Teacher
Government	BA	Raising 4 Children as Doctor's Wife, Various Office Positions
English	BA	Homemaker, Pastor
Theology	M. Div.	
	BA	Education Administration
History and Education	MAT	Lifetime Community Volunteer
Business		Housewife
Business	BS in Commerce and Finance	Information Systems for Insurance Company of North America, Principal System Consultant
		Section Manager in Department Store
Textile merchandising & design		
Fine Arts	BFA	Substitute Teacher, Social Work With Seniors
Art	BA	Taught Art, Art Supervisor, Owned Natural Food Store
Health and Physical Education	BS	Teaching/College Professor, Kutztown University
Health Education	Advanced Graduate Study	

Name	Where Grew up	College or other
Emma Hallman Mele	Souderton, PA	Ursinus
		Drexel Institute of Technology
		Pennsylvania Hospital (Phila.)
Lois Jack Meseroll	Westfield, NJ	New Jersey College for Women, now Douglass College
Martha McGonigle Mewhort	Wyomissing, PA	Duke University
		Boston University
		University of Toledo
Marie Helmmen Moyer	Savanah, GA	Armstrong Jr. College
		Randolph-Macon Women's College
Janeth Mueller	Woodhaven, NY	East Stroudsburg State College
		Hofstra University
Marjorie J. Phillips	Woodhaven, NY	Wilson College, Hunter College, Long Island University and New York University
Amy Howman Reinsel	Wyomissing, PA	Muhlenberg College

Major	Degree	Main Work
		Housewife, Mother, Office Manager, School Nurse
School of Nursing	Registered Nurse	
Economics, Sociology, History	BA	Bell Tel Labs Patent File Clerk, Substitute Teacher, Clerk Glenville State College, Supervisor B Dalton Bookstore, Head Teller
Education, History	BA	History Faculty Lourdes College
	MA	
Psychology		Wife, Mother, Secretary
Sociology	BA	
Health and Physical Education	BS, MS in Education	PE Teacher, Guidance Counselor
Undergraduate: American Civilization, Graduate: History, Counseling	BA, MA, MS, 6th Year Cert. in Counseling	Social Studies Teacher, Guidance Counselor
Psychology/Elementary Education	BA	Elementary Education Teacher, Middle Management in Diakom Lutheran Social Ministries

Name	Where Grew up	College or other
Patricia Ulrich Ritter	Mechanicsburg, PA	Pennsylvania State University
Alice Royer Roy	Paoli, PA	University of Michigan
		University of Maryland
		University of Michigan
Rosanna "Rosie" Hallman Steen	Souderton, PA	Gettysburg College
Marilyn Lusson Turner	Ocean City, NJ	Wagner College
Midge Wilkinson Vansant	Ridgewood, NJ	University of Pennsylvania School of Occupational Therapy
Ruth Clegg Whitsel	Philadelphia, PA	Gettysburg College
		University of North Carolina
Ruth Foedisch Zimmerman	Melrose Park, PA	Russell Sage College
Ruth Foedisch Zimmerman	Melrose Park, PA	Russell Sage College

Major	Degree	Main Work
Home Economics/Retailing	BS	Custom Home Design
English major, French minor	BA	English And Linguistics Professor, California State University, Los Angeles
English literature	MA	
Linguistics	MA, PhD	
Sociology, Music	BS	Wife, Mother, Copy Writer, Taught Tennis in Saudia Arabia
Business and Marketing	BA Business Administration	Housewife and Stay-At-Home Mother
Occupational Therapy		Work with Handicapped Children, Travel Agent
English w/ Education minor	BA	Psychotherapist, Adjunct Instructor at University Of North Carolina
Clinical Social Work	MSW	
Nursing	BS	Nurse, Housewife
Home Economics/Retailing	BS	Custom Home Design
Nursing	BS	Nurse, Housewife

Appendix 6: Biographical Information:

Name	Where Grew up	College or other
Karen Beatty	Bethlehem, PA	Bucknell University, Lehigh University
Barbara Huffman de Belon	Lehighton, PA	Slippery Rock State College, Columbia University Teachers College
Judith Hartman Brewer	Bethlehem, PA	University of Maine
Lenore Townsend Chadwick	Ocean City, NJ	Kent State University, Ball State University, Indiana University, Glassboro State NJ
Diane Shubert Cooke	Devon, PA	Baldwin Wallace College (Berea) Ohio State University
Barbara Dando	Glenside, PA	Ursinus College
Sandra Dempsey	Wynnewood, PA	Centenary College, St. Joseph's University, Bryn Mawr College
Ann Frey	Abington, PA	Connecticut College, Beaver College, Bowling Green University
Jane Grigger		
Nancy Hartman	Bethlehem, PA	University of Delaware, Penn State University, Temple University

Campers of 1960-1970

Major	Degree	Main Work
Sociology and Education	B.S., M.A., M.Ed., Ed.D	Teaching
Health and Physical Education	B.S., M.A., M.Ed., Ed.D	Teaching School, Teaching Community College, Curriculum Development in Business
Political Science and Communications	B.A.	Legislative Director for Members, U.S. House of Representatives
Art Education, Special Education	BS	Teaching Art, Special Education
Elementary School Teacher	BS MA	Elementary School Teacher
English	BA, M Ed	H.S. English Teacher
Psychology, Social Work and Law and Social Policy	BS, MSS, MLSP	Non-Profit Organizations for Preventing Violence Against Women and Children
Mathematics	BA, MA	Quality Engineer/Manager in Manufacturing Environments
Retail Management, School Counseling	BS, M.Ed, Certificate in Family Therapy	H.S. Counselor

Name	Where Grew up	College or other
Nancy Atkiss Haring	Laverock, PA	Temple University
Karen Blickwede Knowlton	Bethlehem, PA	Connecticut College, University of New Hampshire
Molly LeVan	Unknown	
Susan Davit Maxwell	Haverton and Bryn Mawr, PA	Millersville State College
Gay Staudenmaier Moceri	Philadelphia, PA	Upsala College NJ
Anne Dando Oldfield	Glenside, PA	Heidelberg University, Michigan State University
Ann Lentz Partlow	Northampton, PA	Mansfield State College
		Lehigh University
Connie Wiegmann Robinson	suburban Philadelphia, PA	West Chester State College PA, Princeton Theological Seminary
Judy Meseroll Scalzitti	Highland Park, NJ, Glenville, WV	West Virginia University

Major	Degree	Main Work
Elementary Education	BS Education	Mother, Elementary teaching
History, Counseling	BA, M.Ed.	Travel Agent
Elementary Education	Elementary Education BA	Elementary School Teacher
English, Education	BA, Teaching Certificate	Teacher, Supervisor, Curriculum Coordinator, Assistant Principal, Principal
Health and Physical Education	BA, H&PE, MA Education	Teacher, Learning Support Inclusion
Elementary Education	BS in Elementary Education	Teaching
	Masters in Education with Reading Specialist Certificate	Reading Specialist
Elementary Education, Mathematics, Counseling, Theology	B.S., M.Ed., M. Div.	Math Teacher
Recreation Management	B.S.	Marketing, Promotions, Sales and Event Planning

Name	Where Grew up	College or other
Kristine Weckerley Sechler	Easton, PA and New Canaan, CT	Endicott Jr College, Bowling Green State University, University of Toledo OH
Kathy Watson	Drexel Hill, PA	Unknown
Susan Dando Weed	Glenside, PA	Wittenberg University, Beaver College
Dorothy Watson Westgate	Allentown, PA	Skidmore College, Westminster Choir College Princeton
Mary Goldsmith Westhuis	Allentown, PA	Bucknell University, Rutgers University
Carol Feltman Wheeler	Oreland, PA	St. Joseph's University, University of Utah, University of Vermont

Major	Degree	Main Work
Elementary Education	BS Ed, MA Reading Specialist	Teacher, School District Librarian
Pre-School Education	Associate of Arts	Flight Attendant
Elementary Education and Special Education	BA, M ED Montessori Pre-school Special Education	Teacher
Music	B Music	Musician, Typist, Proofreader, Photographer
English, Library and Information Science	BA, MLS	Mother, Librarian
Psychology, School Counseling, Special Education	BS, M. Ed Special Education	School Counselor

Author, with red tie, going home, ten years old

Author's Camp Bio

One of my father's first jobs was as a chauffeur and porter at Shawnee Inn. I was born in East Stroudsburg hospital and lived in Mount Pocono as an infant, so this is my home ground. My father's family was from Northampton and Cherryville, my mother's from Fullerton and Bethlehem, and our family is Pennsylvania Dutch all the way back. I lived a few years in Fullerton, in the house my mother and grandmother were born in. We spent a lot of time in Northampton and environs with my dad's sister and her family, so although I grew up in Paoli, then semi-rural, west of Philadelphia, I think of the Northampton-Poconos area as my other home.

What I like: ring baloney, shoo fly pie, and birch beer. And I am happy to note that a new staff residence in the '60s, called the Barn, had a hex sign on the end.

1945 saw me at age seven in Jr. 2. They said I cried pretty much all day every day, but thankfully I do not remember the experience, nor, unfortunately, the counselor who saw me through it or the counselors of

214

the next two years. In 1947, still a junior, I broke my arm turning cartwheels the length of the long field down between camp and the road, so that season was cut short. Skipper, our well-loved nurse, sat with me until my parents arrived. Ginny Steele, Aquatics (later she would be waterfront head), was my counselor in Int. 6, and I would like to think that was the beginning of my life on waterfront, but in fact I just managed to get into the redcap (beginners) class before I went home, so it was a pretty slow start. Still, it was a big deal to me.

In Sr. 1, with Midge Wilkinson, a waterfront counselor, I finally learned to swim. Once I got the crawl, everything else fell into place and I zipped through the upper cap levels. It was also with Midge that I learned to play the ukelele – what fun that was. Sr. 3, counselor Janie Endres, is the year I was selected to be an Olympics team captain – that remains one of my proudest moments. Inge Woermann was my counselor in Sr. 5. That year I was put on Honor Council, and to this day, there are not many things that have meant so much. My CIT years were spent with Inge, again and happily, and Del (Adele Kocher).

The last two of my years at Hagan, I was counselor first in Int. 9 and then in Sr. 1, when Martie Davis, who initiated the '60s alums' memoir *Make the Rafters Ring!* was in my cabin. At the time of the hurricanes, on my day off in East Stroudsburg, I was one of those, along with Pat Ulrich, who volunteered with the Red Cross, helping evacuate families who lived at the rising water's edge.

At camp I was a non-Lutheran girl, but my family had been Lutheran from forever. I used to say I was a Presbyterian in the winter and a Lutheran in the summer.

I didn't spend a lot of time in Arts and Crafts, no more than the minimum required for whatever tie I was working on. I did enjoy working with wood, and still have the wooden box I made for my father, initials carved on top and finished with shellac and rubbed as close to satin as I could get it. At camp I thought of myself as a swimmer (after I finally learned how) so the Craft Shop was not my favorite place to be. But I learned *so* much – just the image of what was in the Craft Shop and

215

what went on there are all part of my knowledge now.

When I was a CIT, we had a major and minor department where we worked in the daytime. I was a water rat and spent most of my time on the waterfront. My minor was Entertainment, and *minor* is right. I could sing and dance, but I hadn't the faintest idea how to do or teach entertainment. The program succeeded despite me that year. As a camper, I didn't like doing skits very much, but I think now it was part of Hagan's learning: Life gives you a bagful of stuff, make something out of it.

Poison ivy took its toll on many campers at Hagan. On Olympics Day I ran the last leg of the relay race, the final event of the day. I ran like the wind, or so it felt, overran the finish line and fell into the brush at the end of the field – which was full of poison ivy. I had on shorts and a little halter, so I was literally covered with poison ivy, and spent some days in the infirmary, in a smock-sort of housecoat lent by one of my cabin mates (Barbara Kroner) because I couldn't bear to have clothes on my back. Kit Berger, Associate Director, kindly soaked my back with soothing compresses.

Canoeing, which I and most of us loved, provided my other bad encounter with poison ivy. Because of a few mishaps along the way, we made camp late and laid out bedrolls in the dark. The next morning I awoke to three shiny leaves waving over my head. When we set up camp the night before we were wearing the usual bathing suits, sweatshirts, and sneakers without socks, so I had been walking around in poison ivy for a few hours, and you can imagine the rest.

Besides swimming and canoeing, singing was my other great love at Hagan, a lot of it done with Meg Brown and Sue Carmint. We made up harmonies and descants as we went along. Director Janie Endres appointed me Song Leader in 1953 which meant that at campfire I started the songs (planned in the script for the night) at a pitch where I knew everybody could sing each one. I loved walking around the campfire leading rounds like *White Coral Bells*.

My favorite grace was:

216

God has created a new day
Silver and green and gold
Live that the sunset may find us
Worthy his gifts to hold.

My dear friend Ruth speaks for me:

> That grace captured the essence of our life at camp. As we
> left Great Hall, the early sun-filled mornings truly were silver
> and green and gold. From the beginning to the end of the day,
> the program and the relationships of counselor to camper and
> between campers, inspired us to reach inside ourselves and to
> become worthy of our camp's ideals. (adapted)

Camp was where I mainly lived. The rest of the year was stuff that
had to be done, or gone through, until camp started again. There I felt
secure, comfortable, in a place full of friendship and accomplishment. A
life I could live and do mostly right, could understand what was expected
and do it, fit in. And have sisters! As an only child, I was euphoric to
have all those sisters: Ruth Clegg, Pat Ulrich, Nora Ann Ehrig, Elaine
Emenheiser, Meg Brown, Rosie Hallman, Phyl Wiest, Peg Newcomer,
Gloria "Genius" Ryan, and many others, older and younger.

In my life I have spent many years in school in one way or another.
This has taught me, not how wonderful it is to go to school, but how
wonderful it is to learn. After writing and researching for this book, I am
convinced that what really drove Camp Hagan was learning, based on a
child's natural love of learning – how to do, how to be – on the theory
that the human brain, especially that of a child, wants, *needs* to learn. We
rejoice in the beauty of the hills and the river, the joy in friendships, all
powerful elements of Hagan life, ingredients memorialized for us in our
thoughts and images so many years later. But they would not have been
enough without the Hagan day saturated with opportunities to learn, try,
accomplish, and learn some more. How fortunate we were to spend
summers immersed in such a nurturing place. I am grateful.
Alice Royer Roy

Headwaters

Headwaters, as you probably know, are the springs and tributaries that form the start of a river, like the Delaware. The sources that inform this book are the headwaters of our Hagan history.

The *Wooden Album* or *Hagan Scrapbook*

The *Wooden Album*, or the Hagan Scrapbook, is in Christine Hill Killough's words "a marvelous scrapbook maintained and updated lovingly through the years," by directors and associate directors up until 1961. Through the hard work of a team of former campers in 2011 it was found in an old storage shed at Bear Creek, successor to the "river camps," Hagan, and downriver the brother camp, Camp Miller, with Ministerium, the adult and family camp, in between.

The covers of the *Wooden Album* are made of 1/4" plywood, varnished, with the Camp Hagan logo woodburned on the front. The book measures an astonishing 22" long x 11" wide, about three inches thick, and is tied together with a boot lace which was perhaps originally brown and tan. The first page has no writing, but artfully drawn acorns and oak leaves. There are approximately 80 pages, unnumbered, often a two-page spread for a special day such as May Day.

The *Album* contains the hand-signed list of "charter campers" (App.

218

2) and staff, along with photos of campers and staff in 1937 and forward. Director Jane (Tay) Taylor's gentle enthusiasm fills her camp journals for 1938 and '39. There are copies of the Hagan news sheets *The Queue* and the *Hagan Herald* well into the '50s, Christmas banquet programs, photos and many other memoirs.

There is nothing in the album for several years in the '50s but it resumes in 1960, when presumably Director Phyllis Wiest Gilbert finished this brief remainder of the album, ending in 1961.

The Queue

Much of what we know of Camp Hagan's first year comes to us from the daily news sheets called *The Queue*. The originators of *The Queue* recognized that the name would have to be explained. So, on the second day of camp, the writer says of *The Queue:* "according to our dictionary we read that it means a hint. So take a hint from your staff and keep up with the activities of Camp Hagan by reading *The Queue*." The writer seems to have intended *cue*, a hint, rather than *queue*, a line of people. But so it remained for about ten years.

It is unlikely that campers ever understood why the daily news sheet had the name it had. But the little paper was highly informative, alerting the camp of what to plan for and reviewing events from the day before.

And the type! We're looking at typescript from an apparently already old typewriter onto mimeograph paper and then run off for the whole camp. With drawings. A challenging project, carried out nearly every day for the whole season. *The Queue's* 50th birthday was celebrated the beginning of the last week of camp. *The Queue* continued on into the '40s. We are fortunate to have this record of Hagan's first year.

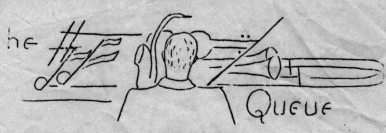

Volume II   August 1, 1938   No. 30

He who Joy would win must share it,
Happiness was born a twin.

FRED WARING MOBBED BY HAGAN GIRLS

Fred Waring and Mr. Brown the manager of Buckwood Inn paid Camp
Hagan a visit Sunday afternoon. The excitement among the campers
was terrific. They discovered who the visitor was and they trailed
him for autographs. Chief Snyder rushed to his rescue, so our young
souvenir hunters were disappointed. Mr. Waring was delighted with
our camp. The cabins pleased him. Great Hall he found con enial
place for work and play. Our waterfront staff in action fascinated
him. We are very gratified at our distinguished visitors pleasure
in us. We are proud of our camp and glad to find ourselves liked.

GET ACQUAINTED PROGRAM SAT. NIGHT

After vespers Saturday evening we gathered in a large friendly
circle in Great Hall for a "sing". Louise helped us to sing our old
songs and taught us some new ones. Our aim was to help the new firls
get into the swim of things as soon as possible . They were soon
singing as loudly as the rest of us. All the counsellors were
introduced all over again. We hope you new girls saw them and will
soon be thoroughly at home with them . They need you in every field
of work. Be sure to look carefully at the daily schedules so that
you know when and where to report for the work you are especially
interested in.

SUGGESTIONS   TO CAMPERS

"Sonny" announces craft specials:
      Rat-trap(Tyrolean felt)belts   Finger painting
      Wooden beading   Wood carving and burning
      Indian beading   Clay modeling and
      Woven peasant belts   sculpture.
   Visit Len at the Shack between 9-10:30 and 2-3:30 to choose
your crafts, then see Sonny and Co. on the porch for instruction
at the periods listed on your schedule.

CHANCE FOR JUNIORS TO SHINE
      Our next big performance is especially suited for Juniors and
Intermediates -- a Musical Show with plenty of dancing and singing.
Louise and Candy want all the Juniors to come out to dancing and
music classes. We need plenty of pretty costumes, too. Show Candy
yours now! Com on Juniors, let's show the Seniors what we can do.

DRAMATIC CLASSES OPEN TO ALL
   Italia needs new acting material for CHRISTMAS! Don't tell us
you didn't know that Aug. 24th is Christmas Eve.

CAMPUS   BITS
Have you heard that Jeanne and Fred Waring are old pals? No, don't
ask Jeanne.

The *Hagan Herald*

Replacing *The Queue* was the *Hagan Herald*, which appeared daily well into the '50s and after that sporadically in the '60s, then seven pages long but unfortunately not dated or numbered. Jane Terry, in charge of the office in 1968, says she worked on an electric typewriter and a ditto machine.

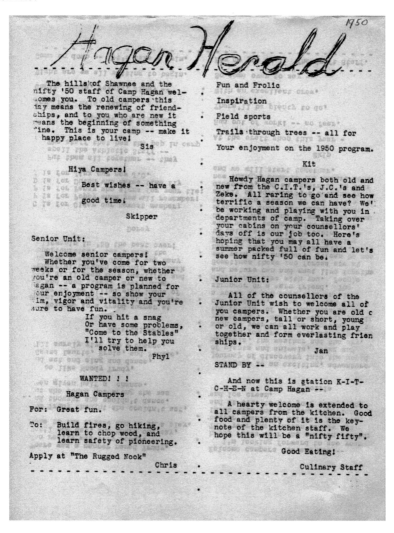

Hagan Herald   1950

The hills of Shawnee and the nifty '50 staff of Camp Hagan welcomes you. To old campers this way means the renewing of friendships, and to you who are new it means the beginning of something fine. This is your camp -- make it a happy place to live!

Sis

Hiya Campers!

Best wishes -- have a

good time!

Skipper

Senior Unit:

Welcome senior campers! Whether you've come for two weeks or for the season, whether you're an old camper or new to Hagan -- a program is planned for your enjoyment -- so show your vim, vigor and vitality and you're sure to have fun.
If you hit a snag
Or have some problems,
"Come to the Stables"
I'll try to help you
solve them.

Phyl

WANTED! ! !

Hagan Campers

For: Great fun.

To: Build fires, go hiking, learn to chop wood, and learn safety of pioneering.

Apply at "The Rugged Nook"

Chris

Fun and Frolic

Inspiration

Field sports

Trails through trees -- all for

Your enjoyment on the 1950 program.

Kit

Howdy Hagan campers both old and new from the C.I.T.'s, J.C.'s and Zeke. All raring to go and see how terrific a season we can have? We'll be working and playing with you in departments of camp. Taking over your cabins on your counsellors' days off is our job too. Here's hoping that you may all have a summer packed full of fun and let's see how nifty '50 can be.

Junior Unit:

All of the counsellors of the Junior Unit wish to welcome all of you campers. Whether you are old or new campers, tall or short, young or old, we can all work and play together and form everlasting friendships.

Jan

STAND BY --

And now this is station K-I-T-C-H-E-N at Camp Hagan --

A hearty welcome is extended to all campers from the kitchen. Good food and plenty of it is the keynote of the kitchen staff. We hope this will be a "nifty fifty".

Good Eating!

Culinary Staff

Sales Brochures

Sales brochures didn't really have a title other than *Camp Hagan for Girls*. Small pamphlets produced by the Synod every year and available to parents on racks in church vestibules or through the minister, they contained a few pictures of the campus or camp life, gave the dates of sessions, the daily schedule, order blanks for uniforms, and, of course, they encouraged parents to send their daughters to Hagan.

Memory Books

Provided to each camper upon arrival, *Memory Books* were kept under the bottom blanket on a Hagan bed. In 1940 the booklet contained advertisements (Glen W. Kisor, Modern Funeral Home, Stroudsburg), "Prayer of a Camper" (*God who touchest earth with beauty*), "The Daily Dozen" (rules and advice), staff list (with a place for each counselor's autograph), Junior and Senior Camp Awards (Crickets and "Whippor- wills," Rangers and Prospectors), songs, places for names of friends and for hours spent in Athletics, Nature, and Music and Dramatics. In 1951, besides the daily schedule, there appeared a list of the synod's Board of Christian Education members and the Executive Staff for the camps, a new "Prayer of a Camper," the list of rules and advice (expanded with extra health advisories), a list of visiting pastors, staff list, space to write

222

in cabinmates, the requirements for all the tie awards, a very small space for a Correspondence Record, and the words to *Taps*. The *Memory Books* remained much the same until 1970.

1948 finally changes from "A Camp With *a* Character" to "A Camp With Character."

The Lutheran *Minutes*

Copies of the Lutheran *Minutes* were collected by Pat Ulrich Ritter and Phyllis Wiest Gilbert at the Lutheran Theological Seminary Philadelphia. The minutes from the Lutheran Synod's annual meeting, reporting on each previous camping season, were named at the beginning of Camp Hagan the minutes of the Annual Convention of the Evangelical Lutheran Ministerium of Pennsylvania and the Adjacent States, changed in 1963 to Minutes of the Proceedings of the Annual Convention of the Eastern Pennsylvania Synod of the Lutheran Church in America.

223

Print Sources

I can't recommend enough Leslie Paris's *Children's Nature* and Abigail Van Slyck's *A Manufactured Wilderness*. Both are scholarly investigations of camping in the late 19th century and the first half of the 20th, both filled with interesting information and photos. Other print sources appear in the Works Cited.

Questionnaires

For this study, two questionnaires were sent to camper/counselors on mailing lists covering all the years of Camp Hagan. Questionnaire I gathered mostly details and numerical data, age upon first going to Hagan, years spent there, staff positions held, and so forth. Questionnaire II asked about experiences, for example canoe trips, mealtimes, singing, hiking.

Sis Wenrich also had used questionnaires in research for her dissertation on making camp-type learning available in elementary schools, and I can only echo her statement that the "enthusiastic response [was a] constant source of inspiration and encouragement" (diss. p. 3).

The questionnaires appear in Appendix 4, along with data about places campers grew up, their education, and their work in Appendixes 5 and 6.

Works Cited

"Building and Repairs to Camp Miller-Hagan-Ministerium According to Synidical Records. Addition to Lutheran Synod *Minutes*." 1927-1966, 1972.

"Camp Miller History." Oct. 23, 2016. <tenlongview.net/Miller/campmillerhist.html>.

Adams, John, and Clayton Alderfe. "Camp Miller History". 1966. April 2, 2014. <http://tenlongview.net/Miller/campmillerhist.html.>.

Adler, Thomas C. *Campingly Yours: A Heartwarming Journey of a Lifetime at Summer Camp*. Chandler, AZ: Five Star Publications, 2009.

Camp Hagan for Girls: Promotional Brochures. 1937 ff.

Dando, Barb, et al. *Make the Rafters Ring! Remembering Camp Hagan*. Indianpolis: Brown Acorn Press, 2015.

Memory Books. 1940 ff.

Minutes of the Proceeding of the Annual Convention of the Evangelical Lutheran Ministerium of Pennsylvania and the Adjacent States. (Until 1963).

Minutes of the Proceedings of the Annual Convention of the Eastern Pennsylvania Synold of the Lutheran Church in America. (After 1963).

Official Blog of Camp Laurel South. "Moosetracks". Casco, Maine. March 8, 2011.

Paris, Leslie. *Children's Nature: The Rise of the American Summer Camp*. New York: NYU Press, 2008.

Postel, Sandra, and Brian Richter. *Rivers for Life: Managing Water for People and Nature*. Washington, DC: Island Press, 2012.

Prell, Riv-Ellen. "Jewish Summer Camping and Civil Rights: How Summer Camps Launched a Transformation in American Jewish Culture". Ann Arbor, MI, 2006. *BELIN LECTURE SERIES*. Jean and Samuel Frankel Center for Judaic Studies the University of Michigan. January 13, 20017.

<http://quod.lib.umich.edu/b/belin/13469761.0013.001?view=text;r gn=main>.

Sargent, Porter. *A Handbook of Summer Camps: An Annual Survey.* Vol. 8: Porter Sargent, 1924.

Shafer, Mary A. *Devastation on the Delaware: Stories and Images of the Deadly Flood of 1955.* Ferndale, PA: Word Forge Books, 2005.

Shukaitis, Nancy Michael. *Lasting Legacies of the Lower Minisink.* East Stroudsburg, PA: Lasting Legacies Books, 2007.

Van Slyck, Abigail A. *A Manufactured Wilderness: Summer Camps and the Shaping of American Youth, 1890-1960.* Minneapolis: University of Minnesota Press, 2006.

this Camp Hagan gal
was created by Kit Berger.
She is wearing Alison Berger
uniform & Bep Berger's
red tie she earned in
1939.
She was sent to Bear
Creek Lutheran camp in
1997 for their archives.
Kit died in 1996. She
made the doll for our
1990 Camp Hagan Reunion
at Moselem Springs Rest.

227

INDEX

Made in the USA
Middletown, DE
05 September 2017